NETS
HOW TO MAKE, MEND
AND PRESERVE THEM

BY

G. A. STEVEN

British Library Cataloguing-in-Publication Data

A catalogue record for this book is available from the
British Library

CONTENTS

ROPE, KNOTS AND NETS 1

PREFACE 7

INTRODUCTION 13

CHAPTER I - A. THE FIRST STEPS 25

CHAPTER II - HOW TO SHAPE A NET .... 53 X

CHAPTER III - SLEEVE NETS, BAG NETS AND SQUARE NETTING .... 71 X

CHAPTER IV - HOW TO MOUNT A NET 102

CHAPTER V - HOW TO MEND 115

CHAPTER VI - ESSENTIAL KNOTS AND HITCHES 134

Overhand knot for joining 2 pieces or starting a fresh needle P135

CHAPTER VII - SOME THINGS TO MAKE 152

CHAPTER VIII - PRESERVATION OF NETS 188

153 string bag for tennis balls
155 Carrying net for football
157 Double ended (both ends closed) carrying bag
162 Shopping bags 3 designs
170 Netball goal
170 Hammock
172 Rabbit (purse) net
175 tennis net
177 different otter trawl nets

Rope, Knots and Nets

A knot is a method of fastening or securing linear material such as rope by tying or interweaving. It may consist of a length of one or several segments of rope, string, webbing, twine, strap, or even chain, interwoven such that the line can bind to itself or to some other object (the 'load'). Knots have been the subject of interest for their ancient origins, their common uses, and the area of mathematics known as knot theory. There is a large variety of knots, each with properties that make it suitable for a range of tasks. Some knots are used to attach the rope (or other knotting material) to other objects such as another rope, cleat, ring, or stake. Some knots are used to bind or constrict objects. Decorative knots usually bind to themselves to produce attractive patterns. While some people can look at diagrams or photos and tie the illustrated knots, others learn best by watching how a knot is tied.

Knot tying skills are transmitted by professions as diverse as sailors, climbers, arborists, rescue professionals, fishermen, linemen and surgeons. Knots can also be applied in combination to produce complex objects such as lanyards and netting – also used for a plethora of different occupations! Netting is one of the key components to fishing in mass quantities. This textile is used because of its sturdy yet flexible origin, which can carry weight yet, still be lightweight and compactable. Fisherman use netting when trawling, because it is sturdy enough to carry large amounts of weight as fish are trapped, pulled, then lifted out of water. Often times, the filaments that make up the yarn are coated with wax or plastic. This coating adds a waterproof component to the textile that provides even more reliability. Using either the Lace-maker or the Net-maker method to tie the netting knot, you can create several types of netting. Diamond mesh netting goes back and forth, in rows; a technique usually used for bags, hammocks, headbands and scarves. Another type is square mesh netting which also goes back and forth in rows but is worked in the diagonal. This type of net is used for trawling; the first row starts at one corner and the last row finishes the corner diagonal to the first corner.

Knot tying consists of the techniques and skills employed in tying a knot in rope, nylon webbing, or other articles. The proper tying of a knot can be the difference between an attractive knot and a messy one, and occasionally life and death. It is therefore incredibly important to understand the often subtle differences between what works, and what doesn't. For example, many knots 'spill' or pull through, particularly if they are not 'backed up', usually with a single or double overhand knot - to make sure the end of the rope doesn't make its way through the main knot, causing

double overhand knot

all strength to be lost. When knotted rope is strained to its breaking point, it almost always fails at the knot or close to it, unless it is defective or damaged elsewhere. The bending, crushing, and chafing forces that hold a knot in place also unevenly stress rope fibres and ultimately lead to a reduction in strength.

The exact mechanisms that cause the weakening and failure are complex, and are the subject of continued study. Common causes are 'slipping' (in which case the load creates tension that pulls the rope back through the knot in the direction of the load. If this continues far enough, the working end passes into the knot and the knot unravels and fails), 'capsizing' (to capsize (or spill) a knot is to change its form and rearrange its parts, usually by pulling on specific ends in certain ways) and 'sliding' (in knots that are meant to grip other objects, failure can be defined as the knot moving relative to the gripped object. While the knot itself does not fail, it ceases to perform the desired function). Relative knot strength, also called knot efficiency, is the breaking strength of a knotted rope in proportion to the breaking strength of the rope without the knot. Determining a precise value for a particular knot is difficult because many factors can affect a knot efficiency test: the type of fibre, the style of rope, size of rope, whether it is wet or dry, how the knot is dressed before loading, how rapidly it is loaded, whether the knot is

capsizing [handwritten marginal note]

repeatedly loaded, and so on.

The efficiency of common knots ranges between 40—80% of the rope's original strength. In most situations forming loops and bends with conventional knots is far more practical than using rope splices, even though the latter can maintain nearly the rope's full strength. Prudent users allow for a large safety margin in the strength of rope chosen for a task due to the weakening effects of knots, aging, damage, shock loading, etc. The working load limit of a rope is generally specified with a significant safety factor, up to 15:1 for critical applications. For life-threatening applications, other factors come into play. The list of knots is extensive, but common properties allow for a useful system of categorization. Common types of knots are 'Bend' (a knot uniting two lines), 'Binding' (a knot that restricts objects by making multiple winds), 'Hitch' (a knot tied to a post, cable, ring or spar), 'Slip' (a knot tied with a hitch around one of its parts. In contrast, a loop is closed with a bend, and while a slip knot can be closed, a loop remains the same size), 'Splice' (a knot formed by interweaving strands or rope rather than whole lines — more time consuming but usually stronger than simple knots) and finally, 'Whipping' (a binding knot used to prevent another line from fraying).

20 MM

1

2

3

4

5

6

7

8

9   3MM

10 4MM
    Mono Jute

11 5MM

12 6MM

8MM

Size-chart showing thicknesses of cotton and hemp twines

10 MM

14MM

PREFACE

OF the making of books there is said to be no end. Nevertheless, no apology is needed for adding this one to their number. Time and again, over a period of many years, I have been asked to recommend a good book on net-making and net-mending. Invariably I have had to reply that, to the best of my knowledge, no such book exists in the English language—or, for that matter, in any other language. A few publications, long since out of print and unobtainable, deal with the subject in such a superficial way that, even if they were still available, they would be of little use. The brief references to net-making that are to be found in most of the current books on knots, ties and splices, and in at least one well-known treatise on needlework, extend to only a few paragraphs or a few pages at most, and not much can be learned from them. Some slightly fuller accounts have lately become available but those that I have seen appear to have been written by amateurs for amateurs and cannot be recommended to anyone seriously interested in the subject.

Much netting is now factory-made by very elaborate machinery; but manual braiding is still an essential accomplishment wherever nets are used, and no net can be properly mended in any other way than by hand. This book deals with manual methods only, and is offered to professionals and amateurs alike. It is so planned and presented that anyone who has never before handled or even seen a netting needle should be able in a few days to make a simple rectangular piece of flat netting. The learner is then led step by step to the more difficult parts of the subject and should have no difficulty in mastering them provided that he possesses and uses the three attributes that are as essential for success in this as in everything else—patience, perseverance, practice.

Professional net-makers will be already familiar with much of the contents of the book; but even they, I think, will find described within its pages methods that are new to them. I believe this to be so because some were quite unknown to me until I learned them from native fishermen in various British colonies. I cannot name all those fishermen individually. Indeed it would be perhaps of little use for few of them can read or write. Nevertheless, though they may never know it, I must place on record my deep gratitude for all that they taught me, for their unfailing kindness always; and, as I got to know them better, for their true friendship as well.

It is with pleasure that I acknowledge also much helpful interest and advice from the Gourock Rope-work Co., Ltd. (Plymouth branch); the Great Grimsby Coal, Salt and Tanning Co., Ltd. (Newlyn branch); and Messrs. Joseph Gundry & Co., Ltd., Bridport. Hints and criticisms from individuals have been legion but I am particularly indebted to Skippers W. J. Creese and W. E. Nichols, of Plymouth, and to Skipper W. J. Tiller, of Brixham, for many invaluable suggestions. Most of all, perhaps, I owe to Skipper R. E. Brown, of Hull, who was my colleague on fisheries development duties during difficult times in British West Africa. His vast knowledge of all appertaining to the making, mending and handling of fishing nets was always freely and liberally at my disposal and I learned much from him. Finally, I must express my particular indebtedness to Miss Jean Millen Adam, of Glasgow, who, with great skill and care, transferred my original drawings to bristol board and put them into proper shape for reproduction. Without her aid I doubt if this book would ever have reached completion.

G.A.S. Plymouth, June, 1949.

9

NETS
HOW TO MAKE, MEND
AND PRESERVE THEM

INTRODUCTION

A PIECE of netting is easy to recognise and hard to define. According to the *Encyclopaedia Britannica*[1] "a net consists of a fabric of thread, twine, or cord, the intersections of which are firmly knotted so as to form meshes or interspaces of fixed dimensions,—the meshes being usually lozenges of uniform size."

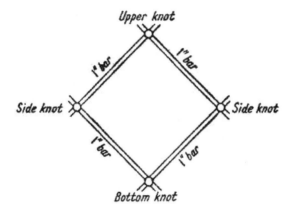

FIG. 1.

A normal mesh has four sides or "bars" of equal length (Fig. 1), and it is the length of the bar that determines the size of the mesh. To state the length of a bar is therefore the best way of describing the size of a mesh. Unfortunately, amongst

13

the makers and users of nets, this method is not everywhere adopted. For example, a piece of netting having one-inch bars may be described in any of the following ways:—[1]

1. One-inch bar—i.e., the length of each side of any mesh is one inch (Fig. 1).

2. Two-inch mesh—i.e., the distance between the top and bottom knots of any mesh is two inches when the knots are drawn fully apart, so that the mesh opening is closed and the side knots are in contact. In other words, the length of a fully stretched mesh is two inches (Fig. 2).

3. Thirty-six "rounds"[2] to the yard (or twelve rounds to one foot) of fully stretched net.

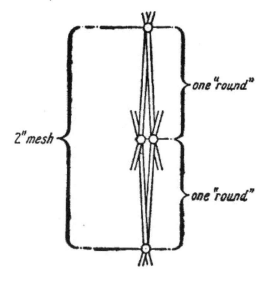

FIG. 2.

4. The size of gauge used to make the net may be given.

Method 2 is the cause of much confusion because "mesh" is often taken to mean "bar." It is therefore strongly recommended that this method be totally discarded and that methods 1 and 3 be universally adopted. Method 1 is the more convenient when applied to meshes of large size, and method 3 should be used for small-meshed nets. Method 4, though unambiguous, is not recommended because it is not readily adaptable to general use.

FIG. 3.

The usual term applied to the making of nets by hand is "braiding." Almost any kind of rope, twine, cord, string, and even some kinds of hair can be made up into netting.[1] Very few tools are required, and these are of the simplest. They consist of needles and mesh-sticks or gauges. These can easily be made at home from pieces of wood with the aid of a pocket-knife, or bought for a few pence at a marine store in any fishing port.

FIG. 4.

The material from which a net is to be made must be wound round a needle of suitable size of which there are two kinds, illustrated in Figs. 3 and 4. The type illustrated in Fig. 3 is the one most generally used for all but very fine work. Near the pointed end there is an opening or "eye" with a "tongue" projecting forwards into it. The other end has two prongs. The needle illustrated in Fig. 4 has no eye and tongue; it is provided at both ends with relatively long curved prongs with their tips nearly meeting.

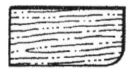

FIG. 5.

FIG. 6.

FIG. 7.

The size of the meshes is regulated by forming them over a mesh-stick or gauge (Figs. 5, 6, and 7). A different gauge is required for each size of mesh so it is a good plan to have a representative series ready to choose from for any particular job. If made at home the gauges will usually consist of wood. Any close-grained wood will do, beech being particularly suitable. The writer always uses home-made gauges of the type illustrated in Fig. 5. The following is a suitable range for most purposes but it can be altered to suit special requirements:—

	length		*width*		*thickness*	*for meshes of*
i.	4 in.	×	¾ in.	×	¼ in.	1-in. bar
ii.	4 in.	×	1 in.	×	¼ in.	1¼-in. bar
iii.	4½ in.	×	1¼ in.	×	¼ in.	1½-in. bar
iv.	4½ in.	×	1¾ in.	×	¼ in.	2-in. bar
v.	4½ in.	×	2¼ in.	×	¼ in.	2½-in. bar
vi.	5 in.	×	2¾ in.	×	¼ in.	3-in. bar
vii.	5 in.	×	3¼ in.	×	¼ in.	3½-in. bar
viii.	6 in.	×	3¾ in.	×	¼ in.	4-in. bar
ix.	6 in.	×	4¾ in.	×	¼ in.	5-in. bar
x.	7 in.	×	5½ in.	×	½ in.	6-in. bar

When using gauges of this pattern the length of a bar will be roughly equal to the width plus the thickness of the gauge.[1] Gauges for meshes outside this range of sizes will generally be of different length and thickness. They may be bought ready-made and will then usually consist of some light metal such as one of the aluminium alloys. In order to reduce weight still further a piece is often cut out of the centre (Fig. 6). This opening has no other use. All the gauges should have one corner rounded off as shown in the illustrations. When in use, the rounded corner lies in the palm of the left hand where it fits more comfortably than a sharp corner would do. Some net-makers prefer gauges shaped as in Fig. 7. In this case the length of a bar will be half the girth of the gauge.

When buying twines for practice and for making the different articles described in Chapter VII of this book, it will be useful to furnish samples of the twines that are wanted. Often this cannot be done and one's requirements must be stated in words. The kinds and quantities offer no difficulty but it is less easy to express in simple language the sizes that are needed because the designation of twine thickness (generally spoken of as "size") is rather complicated and difficult to understand. An exhaustive explanation of the subject is beyond the scope of this book but a brief account of the most important principles is necessary and will be found useful by all users of twines.

Let us begin with cotton twines. The original cotton fibres, suitably prepared, are twisted together into long threads or yarns that are then further twisted together to form the finished twine. Twines differ from one another in both the number and the thickness of the yarns they contain. These two variables are expressed in figures—e.g., 32/12 ply. The first part of the specification (32) is known as the "count" and signifies the size of the yarn used in making up the twine; the second number (12) signifies the "ply"—i.e., the number of yarns. Thus 32/12 ply cotton twine means that 12 yarns of 32 count have been used in making it. Similarly with 10/9, 12/8, 36/6, 40/12 and so on.

No. 1 count indicates a yarn of such size that 840 yds. of it weigh one pound. This is a universal basis or constant to which the sizes of all other cotton yarns (the counts) are related. Thus a count of 32 indicates a yarn so thin that 32 hanks each of 840 yds, would be required to weigh one pound; in other words one pound of this yarn would be $840 \times 32 = 26,880$ yds. long. A count of 40 indicates a still thinner yarn a pound of which would be $840 \times 40 = 33,600$ yds. long. Thus the count number increases as the yarn size diminishes. From the count and the ply the "yardage" of finished twine—i.e., the number of yards to the pound—is easily calculated. Again, taking 32/12 ply as an example, the length of twine in a pound will be the constant (840) multiplied by the count (32) and divided by the ply (12) which gives a length of 2240 yds.

19

Of course, this is only an approximate result as some length is lost when the twist is put in, but it is accurate enough for all practical purposes.

The final size of all twines is determined by both the yarn count and the ply. Therefore two twines having the same count but different ply numbers will be different sizes. Thus 32/9 ply cotton is a little thinner than 32/12 ply; but 12/12 ply is much thicker than 32/12 ply.

$$32/9 \text{ ply} \rightarrow \frac{32 \times 840}{9} = 2{,}897 \text{ yds. to a pound.}$$

$$32/12 \text{ ply} \rightarrow \frac{32 \times 840}{12} = 2{,}240 \text{ yds. to a pound.}$$

$$12/12 \text{ ply} \rightarrow \frac{12 \times 840}{12} = 840 \text{ yds. to a pound.}$$

By similar simple yardage calculations a good idea of the sizes of different twines is easily obtainable.

In practice the yarns are generally laid up into three or four main strands before they are finally twisted together to form the finished twine. Thus 32/12 ply twine may consist of either three strands each containing four yarns of 32 count or of four strands each comprising three yarns.

The specifications of hemp and flax twines are similar to those of cotton except that the standard basis or count is a "lea" of 300 yds. to the pound. Yardage calculations can likewise be made in the same way as for cotton. Unfortunately, different manufacturers often use their own trade numbers for designating the different twine sizes, and as there is no uniformity amongst them much confusion has resulted which could easily have been avoided.

In order to assist beginners to obtain from any shop or firm the size of cotton and hemp twines they require a size-chart is provided as a frontispiece to this book. Twelve different thicknesses are shown. Many more are included in the full range of twines available on the market but those shown here are sufficiently representative for most purposes. Before ordering new twine, a piece of string or twine of about the correct thickness should be placed, tightly stretched, on the black lines of the chart until the best match is obtained. The number should then be noted and an order placed accordingly, reference being made to this book. In the instructions that follow (Chapter VII) for making various netted articles the specifications of cotton and hemp twines are given in terms of the numbered sizes shown on the frontispiece chart.

Fortunately there is a fair measure of uniformity in specifying the sizes of manila and sisal twines. The raw fibres of both those materials are relatively long, besides being too coarse to be made up into yarns. They are therefore made up directly into strands, three or four of which are further twisted together to form the finished twine. Manila and sisal twines

21

are therefore designated by the number of strands they contain and the length in yards that goes to a pound. The yardage of the twines in normal circulation varies from 75 to 225 yds. to the pound. Two examples of twines at present in common use for fishing purposes are "sisal[1] four ply, 100's" and "sisal three ply, 125's."

[1] Ninth edition.

[1] And some others that need not be mentioned.

[2] A "round" is a line of half-meshes—i.e., the distance between consecutive rows of knots when the meshes are fully stretched. If, in counting a number of rounds, the first or last round, but not both, is included, the number of rows of knots will be the same as the number of rounds of half-meshes. If neither the first nor the last round is included in the count, the number of rows of knots in any given length will be one more than the number of rounds. These measurements are generally made at right angles to the head and foot of a piece of netting and not parallel to them (see Fig. 39, I–V).

[1] The various kinds of wire nets do not consist of "netting" in the strict sense of the term as used here.

[1] Actually there may be a slight discrepancy but it is of no importance.

[1] For most purposes, including fishing, sisal is inferior to manila and is used only when manila is unobtainable.

CHAPTER I

A. THE FIRST STEPS

General Principles

For practice purposes the beginner should braid a plain rectangular piece of flat netting twelve meshes wide and as long as he cares to make it. To commence or "set up" the net a short piece of twine, the *foundation line*, strong but not too thick, is stretched taut between two supports. On this foundation line a "round" (row) of twelve loops or half-meshes is made (Fig. 8). This is done by forming a series of thirteen clove hitches (Fig. 13, p. 12) along it, working from right to left,[1] a loop of twine being made to hang down between each pair of clove hitches.

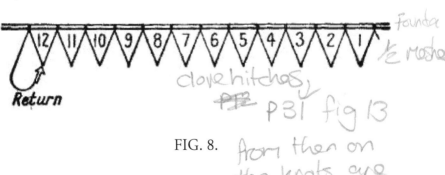

FIG. 8.

25

A second round of half-meshes is now made, working
back from left to right as indicated by the arrow in Fig. 8.
Clove hitches are no longer used; the knots from now on are
sheet bends (Figs. 26 and 27) made on the tips of the loops
of the preceding round of half-meshes. This completes the
first series of twelve full meshes, and the third round of half-
meshes is formed on round 2, working this time from right to
left again (Fig. 9). It will be noticed that, although it required
two rounds of working to produce the first series of complete
meshes, an extra series of complete meshes is formed by round
3 and every succeeding round (Fig. 10). This is because every
round, except the first or "setting-up" round, closes the half-
meshes between the lower halves of the fully formed meshes
in the previous round. Round after round can be added in
this way indefinitely until any desired length of netting is
produced.

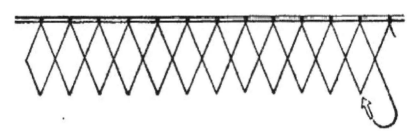

FIG. 9.

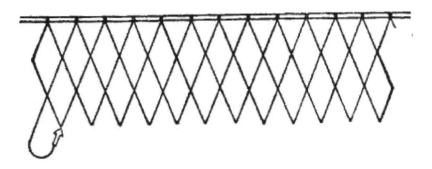

FIG. 10.

From this description of what to do let us now proceed to a detailed study of how to do it.

Loading the Needles

The needle illustrated in Fig. 3 is "loaded" or "filled" in the following manner. Hold the needle in the left hand, point uppermost. Place the free end of the twine on one side of it under the left thumb (Fig. 11); then up and around the tongue, down the same side (over the top of the free end of the twine) and around the bottom between the prongs. Now turn the needle and lead the twine up the other side, round the tongue and down again (Fig. 12)—and so on until the needle is filled. The twine should be kept taut and pulled firmly into position during the filling process so that a tidy and compact "load" is formed.

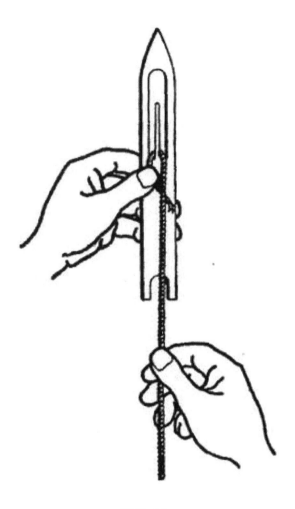

FIG. 11.

The method of filling the second type of needle is obvious; the twine is simply led round and round it lengthways and between the prongs at each end until the needle is fully loaded.

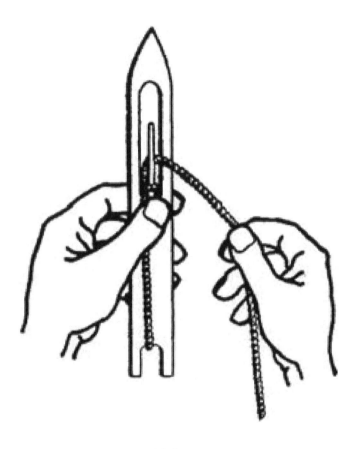

FIG. 12.

[1] The expert net-maker can make the knots right-to-left
or left-to-right as he pleases. The left-to-right method is best
for the beginner as this makes it easier to form the second
round.

B. SETTING-UP

Flat Netting—Method 1

Having provided yourself with a loaded needle take up a position in front of the stretched foundation line already mentioned. Since your piece of netting is to be twelve meshes wide, thirteen clove hitches (Fig. 13) must be formed on this line with twelve loops hanging down between them (Fig. 8). This is done as follows. From the loaded needle, held in the right hand, unwind about one foot of twine which is held in the left hand between index finger and thumb, a few inches from the free end. Then pass the needle away from you, over the line and down underneath it until the needle reaches a position opposite the front of the left hand (Fig. 14). Now draw the needle towards you and upwards in the direction of the left shoulder (Fig. 15) until the left hand (which maintains a non-slip grip on the twine) is brought up close to the foundation line where it will be possible to grip the two parts of the netting-twine between the first finger and thumb of the left hand, thus forming a tight loop or half-hitch over the foundation line (Fig. 16). With the twine held firmly in the left hand, the needle is now carried away from you, over the line again, and then towards you, underneath it, at the back of the left hand. These motions, if properly performed, make a loop of twine at the back of the left hand through which the needle is passed (Fig. 17). This completes the first clove hitch which is now pulled tight (Fig. 13).

FIG. 13.

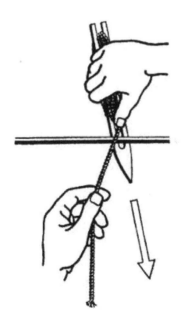

FIG. 14.

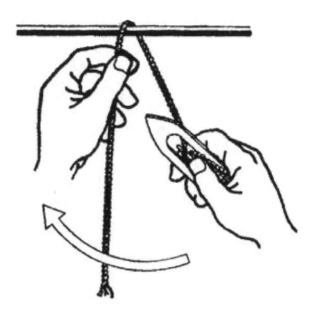

FIG. 15.

FIG. 16.

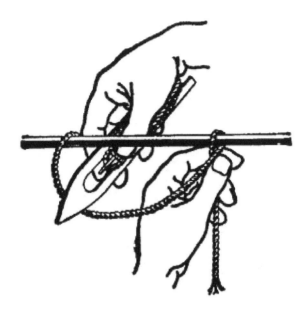

FIG. 17.

A loop of the required size is now made over the left hand fingers[1] and a second clove hitch is made to the left of the first one, in the same way as before (Fig. 18). Proceeding in this way, thirteen clove hitches are made on the line with twelve equal-sized loops or half-meshes between them (Fig. 8).

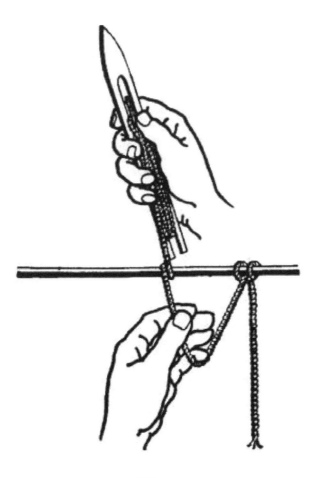

FIG. 18.

Although it is generally best to make the first row of half-meshes over one's fingers in this way, some workers prefer to use a gauge as shown in Fig. 19. After the first round, a gauge *must* be used in order to obtain meshes of uniform size.

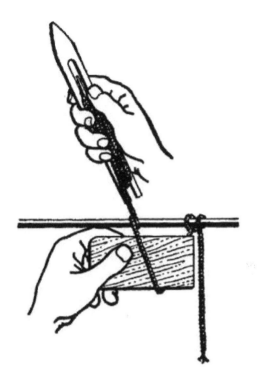

FIG. 19.

The second row of half-meshes is now commenced, working from left to right this time. The knots, as we know, henceforth are to be sheet bends, formed on the tips of the loops or half-meshes already completed. Holding the gauge in the left hand a little way below loop 12—i.e., the last half-mesh of the setting-up round—bring the needle down in front of it, up behind it, and then up through the loop, from the far side towards you (Fig. 20). Now pull the needle strongly towards you until the upper edge of the gauge is brought hard

35

up against the tip of loop 12 (Fig. 21). Where the twine comes forward over the edge of the gauge grip it and the tip of loop 12 firmly between the thumb and first finger of the left hand and hold them securely in that position pressed tightly against the upper edge of the gauge (Fig. 22). Now with a clockwise swing of the right hand, indicated by the arrow ribbon, cause the working part of the twine—i.e., the part between the gauge and the needle—to form a loop lying above and to the left of the left hand. Then pass the needle behind both bars of half-mesh 12 and out through the loop already formed in the working part of the twine (Fig. 23). Then pull tight and a sheet bend is formed such as is illustrated in Fig. 26 on p. 20.

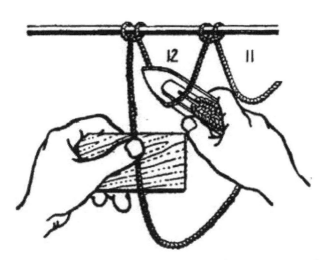

FIG. 20. Sheet bends

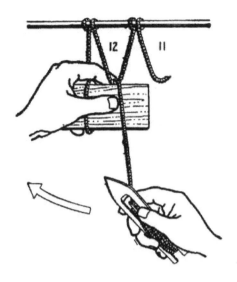

FIG. 21.

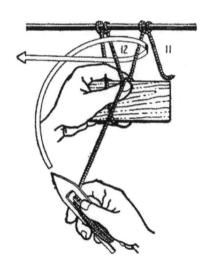

FIG. 22.

After the first mesh is completed others of the second round are formed, one after the other, in the same way, the newly-formed loops lying side by side around the gauge and a row of knots along the top. As new half-meshes are formed over the right-hand end of the gauge, previouly formed ones are allowed to slip off it over the left-hand end held in the left palm. In this way the whole round can be made without any pause to clear the gauge which is only completely removed from the loops when the end of the round is reached.

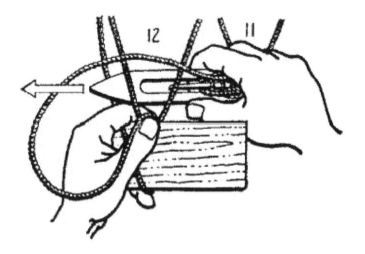

FIG. 23.

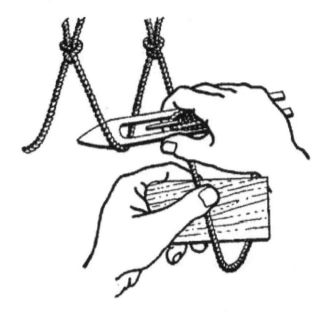

FIG. 24.

Next comes round 3. This must be worked from right to left. The beginning of this round is shown in Fig. 24. Note carefully that, when braiding in this direction, the needle is passed *down* through the loop of the half-mesh of the previous round in the direction away from you—i.e., over the right-hand side of the loop and under the left-hand side. This is clearly shown in the illustration. Apart from this difference there is no other change in the formation of the knot, and a row of half-meshes is formed over the gauge, from the right-hand end, as before (Fig. 25).

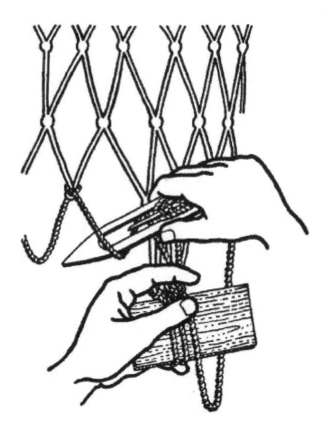

FIG. 25.

Some workers find it easier to make "left-to-right" rounds than to make "right-to-left" ones. They therefore set up their foundation line in a place where there is room to stand on both sides of it. Then, after completing round 2 from left to right, they move to the other side of the line and face it from the opposite direction. What previously was the right-hand edge of the net now becomes "left" again and the next round is made in the usual left-to-right manner. In this way, by changing sides after every round, no alteration need be made in the way the needle, is passed through the loops—i.e., it is brought *up* through them from the far side towards you, every time.

This method is not recommended. Where, as is usual on board ship, one has to work in a confined space, it is seldom possible to stretch a foundation line in such a way that there is room to face it from both sides. Usually the foundation line is strung between two convenient points on a bulkhead where the worker can face it from one side only. There is no alternative, therefore, to working each round from left to right and right to left alternately. It is best, therefore, to learn to braid in this way from the very outset. Moreover, when mending a hole in a large net the work cannot be done from different sides—there is too much net in the way. Here again it is necessary to work from left to right and right to left alternately, passing the needle through the meshes in the proper direction as required. If this is not done, twisted meshes will result. A properly made knot, when working a left-to-right round, appears as in Fig. 26. The knots in a right-to-left round appear as in Fig. 27. If, however, the needle is not passed through the meshes in the correct direction, the bars of the previous half-mesh become crossed as illustrated in Fig. 28. This cannot be corrected by turning the knot over; that simply results in transferring the "twist" to the bars of the next half-mesh below. In nets made of very fine twine the formation of such "twisted meshes" is not of any great importance. In those made of thick twine, however, such twisting may significantly alter the size of the meshes, besides spoiling their appearance.

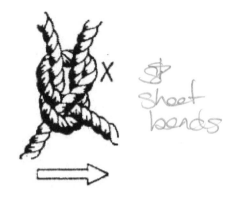

FIG. 26.

FIG. 27.

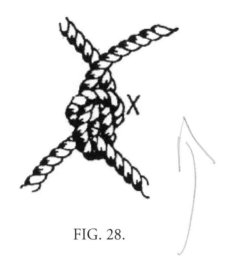

FIG. 28.

While the knots are being pulled tight care must be taken to ensure that the part marked "X" in Figs. 26, 27 and 28 is not allowed to slip down, past the tip of the loop on which it is forming, into the position shown in Fig. 29. If tightened in that position a sheet bend is not formed: merely the useless knot shown in Fig. 30.

FIG. 29.

FIG. 30.

In practice, when setting up a net on a stretched foundation line, the clove hitches are made close together and the first round appears as illustrated in Fig. 31. With the partially closed loops thus formed it is easier to get an even pull on the twine when forming the knots of the next round and a more uniform result is obtained.

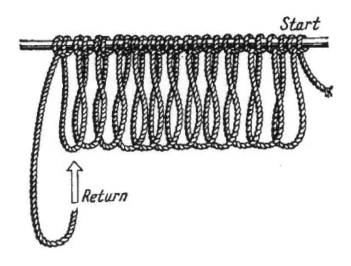

FIG. 31.

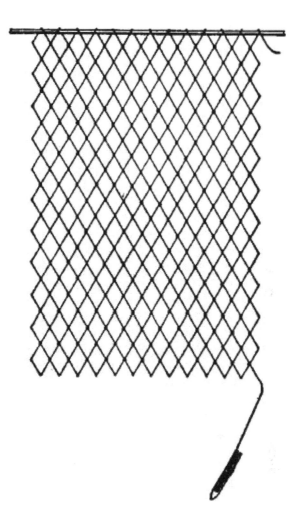

FIG. 32.

On completion of the first few rounds many workers remove the foundation line. The clove hitches then disappear and the first row of half-meshes is set free. They are then rove on to another line (Fig. 32), or on to a rod, and braiding continued in the usual way. With the disappearance of the clove hitches the half-meshes in the original round become slightly enlarged. This is generally of no importance. If, however, it should be essential to keep the first row of half-meshes exactly the same size as those in the remainder of the net, allowance must be made for this in setting up.

FIG. 33.

After a sufficient length of net has been made (Fig. 32) it can be turned over after every round and worked continuously from left to right without changing sides (Fig. 33).

Flat Netting—Method 2   *chaining out*

Some net-makers prefer to dispense with the stretched foundation line when starting or setting up a net and use quite another method known as "chaining out." In some ways this method is preferable to the "foundation line" one.

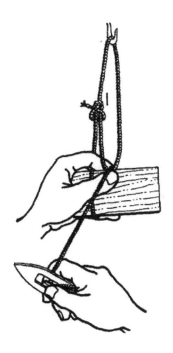

FIG. 34.

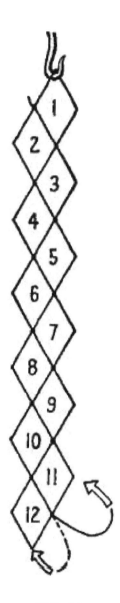

FIG. 35.

Using a bowline or other non-slip knot, make a loop on the end of the twine the size of one complete mesh. Hang this *foundation mesh* (mesh 1) on a convenient nail or hook and arrange it so that the knot is half-way up the left-hand side (Fig. 34). Then, using the appropriate gauge, make another mesh on the foundation mesh. This is mesh No. 2, and the knot will be on the right. When completed, and the knot pulled tight, remove the gauge, and turn the work over so that the knot just made is now towards the left. Then, in the same way as before, make mesh 3 on the tip of mesh 2. In this way, by reversing the chain after every mesh so as always to have the last completed knot on the left, make a series of rounds of one mesh each (Fig. 35). Continue until there are twice as many meshes in the chain as are required in the width of the net to be made. Thus a chain of twelve meshes is required for a net six meshes wide. Note how these meshes are numbered in the illustration. The original or foundation mesh (No. 1) is now lifted off the hook and the *even*-numbered meshes, which now form the first row of meshes of the net, are rove or laced[1] on to a line or rod in the usual manner. When this is done further braiding is continued in the normal way (Fig. 36). It should be noticed that the first two rows of knots are at right angles to all the others in any net "set up" in this way. This may sometimes cause a little trouble when mending.[2]

49

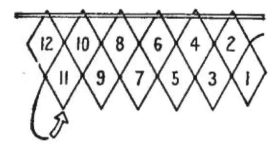

FIG. 36.

Flat Netting—Method 3

Make a large independent loop of suitable *spare* twine and hang it up on a convenient hook. This is the *foundation loop*. Then take a loaded needle and knot the free end of its twine on to the tip of this foundation loop using a simple overhand knot (see Fig. 119, p. 82). This is the starting knot (Fig. 37S). Now, using the appropriate gauge, complete a half-mesh making the usual sheet bend netting knot. The method is fully illustrated in the figure. Continue making half-meshes on the foundation loop in this way and the result will be as illustrated in Fig. 38 with a series of loops (half-meshes) around the gauge and a row of knots along the top of it. Continue until as many loops have been made as the number of meshes that are required in the width of the net. Then remove the gauge, turn the work right over, and make a second round of half-meshes in the usual manner. Carry on in this way, round upon round, until the required length of netting has been made.

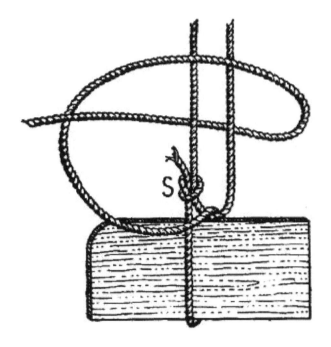

FIG. 37.

It is generally an advantage, after a few rounds have been completed, to untie the starting knot and pull out the foundation loop, cutting it if necessary. The first row of knots then disappears and the free meshes are rove on to a line or rod as previously described. Then carry on braiding as long as necessary to complete the net.

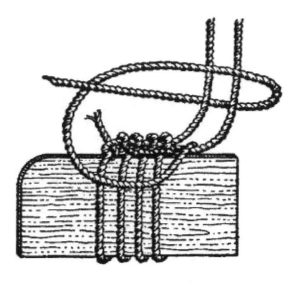

FIG. 38.

[1] Some or all the fingers may be used, depending upon the size of loop to be made.

[2] In Fig. 35 the dotted line and arrow indicate how the work would have been continued if a wider net were to be made. The continuous line and arrow indicate how the working will go after the even meshes are transferred to a rod as in Fig. 36.

CHAPTER II

HOW TO SHAPE A NET

Some Definitions

There is little difficulty in setting-up and making a simple rectangular piece of flat netting, which is all that has been described thus far. It is in shaping a piece of net to fulfil some particular requirement that skill and care are chiefly needed. Before explaining how this is done it is necessary that we should know the appropriate terms used in describing nets and their parts.

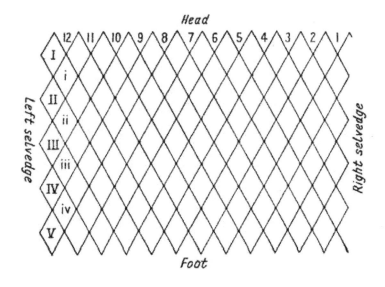

FIG. 39.

Let us assume that, on the original twelve half-meshes we set up (Fig. 8, p. 9), we have made nine rounds of half-meshes or, in other words, that we have made a rectangular piece of netting twelve meshes wide and ten rounds deep (Fig. 39). The edge of the net where it was started is known as the "head"; that where it was finished is the "foot"; the two side edges are the "selvedges" or "selvages."

If we now examine our piece of net we shall find that, although there are ten rounds of half-meshes in its depth, there are only nine rows of knots—i.e., the number of rounds in the complete net is one more than the number of rows of knots. This is because the first row of starting clove hitches disappeared when the line on which the net was originally set up was pulled out.

This does not apply to any piece of netting that includes neither the starting nor the finishing round. Looking again at our piece of netting (Fig. 39) we shall see that ten rounds of half-meshes produce a depth of five full meshes (I–V) and four full meshes (i–iv) in alternate vertical lines along its width, and that there are twelve of each. That is to say, there are (12 × 5) + (12 × 4) = 60 + 48 = 108 full meshes in the net. This is 12 less than 12 × 10 but the discrepancy is accounted for by the fact that there are twelve half-meshes along the head of the net and twelve at its foot which, being the equivalent of twelve full meshes, make up the correct number.

It is interesting to notice that there would have been no difference in the number of meshes in alternate lines from head to foot in our piece of netting if we had made it eleven rounds deep; the number would have been five in each case. The total number of full meshes would then have been (12 × 5) + (12 × 5) full meshes plus 24 half-meshes = 60 + 60 + 12 = 132 (i.e., 12 × 11) full meshes.

In describing the depth of a net it is usual to refer to the number of full meshes in one vertical line from head to foot— i.e., half the number of rounds, disregarding the extra row if the number is odd. Thus, a piece of netting having ten rounds is five meshes deep, and a piece having eleven rounds is also five meshes deep.

Straight Selvedges

Turning yet again to our piece of netting (Fig. 39) and examining its selvedges we see that the outer tips of the end meshes in every alternate row hang free. These are normal selvedges, and they have an uneven and rather untidy appearance. It is therefore often an advantage to have a straight selvedge at one or both edges of a piece of net. This is done by taking up the long arm of the first mesh of every round in its own knot (Fig. 40).* The selvedges will then appear as in Fig. 41. These are also known as double selvedges; they increase the strength of a net at its edges.

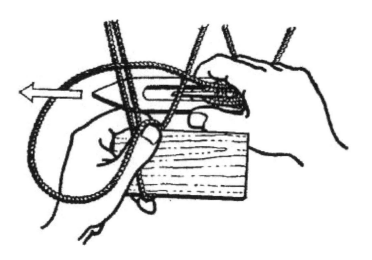

FIG. 40.

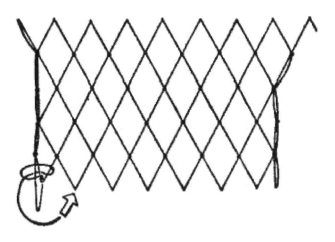

FIG. 41.

Bating

The shape of a piece of flat netting may be altered by bringing about a slope in one or both of its sides. This is done by altering the number of meshes in successive rounds. The number may be either decreased or increased, and the process is known as "bating"[1] and "creasing" respectively.

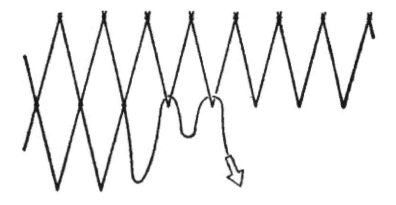

FIG. 42.

To "bate" or reduce the number of meshes in any round it is merely necessary to pick up two half-meshes of the previous round in a single knot of the round that is being made. This is done by passing the needle first through one half-mesh and then through the next one beyond it (Fig. 42) before proceeding with the formation of the knot in the normal way (Fig. 43). Bating should be done not in the middle of the round but near the selvedge that is to be sloped. If the net is to be strongly sloped a bating will be made in every round; lesser slopes are made by bating in every second, third or fourth round and so on.

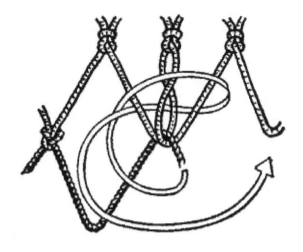

FIG. 43.

Fly-meshing

For certain purposes it is best to have neither a normal nor a straight selvedge but to have a series of fly-meshes down the edge. This method, known as fly-meshing, consists in missing out the last mesh of the previous round (Fig. 44). It is not usual to fly-mesh both selvedges but this can be done if any special purpose demands it. Fly-meshing one selvedge results in reducing the width by one mesh in every other round. It is thus the equivalent of losing one half of one mesh in every round.

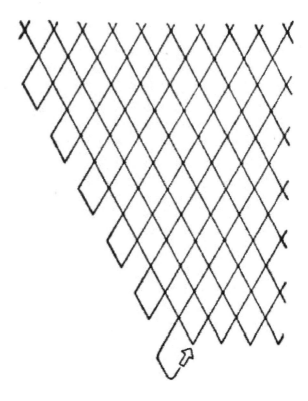

FIG. 44.

Where special strength is required in fly-meshes—as in the wing portions of fishing trawls—they should be doubled. This is done by doubling the first mesh of each returning round—i.e., the mesh that will become the fly-mesh in the next round. The method is as follows: After making the first return mesh in the usual way carry the needle up to the last knot of the previous round and make another knot (Fig. 45). This doubles one side. Then continue the return round as before, thus doubling the remainder of the mesh (Fig. 46). There will be a double knot at *a* and *b* in each fly-mesh.

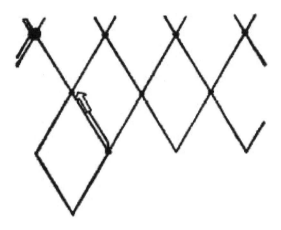

FIG. 45.

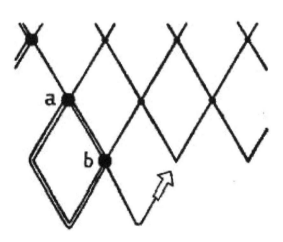

FIG. 46.

Bating by Doubling

There is another good method of sloping the edge of a net at the same rate as fly-meshing—i.e., a reduction of one mesh in every other round—but keeping a straight selvedge in which the marginal meshes are strengthened by doubling. The method is known as the "doubling" method of bating. It is carried out in the following manner.

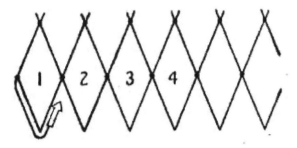

FIG. 47.

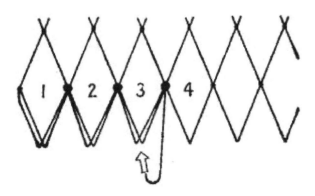

FIG. 48.

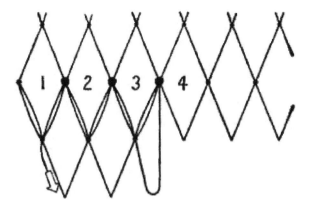

FIG. 49.

On the completion of any round double over the last few meshes, say three, at the edge to be sloped (Fig. 47)—though any number can be doubled—and return to the selvedge (Fig. 48). This makes two normal single meshes and one long-armed mesh (Fig. 49). Return again, doubling over the first two normal meshes by picking up meshes 2 and 3 of the previous round. Then carry on normally to mesh 4 of the previous round, and pick up the long-armed mesh in the knot. Fig. 50 shows this being done and Fig. 51 illustrates the knot drawn tight. Inspection of the illustration will show that this reduces the breadth of the net at the rate of one mesh in every other round.

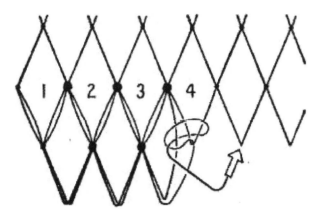

FIG. 50.

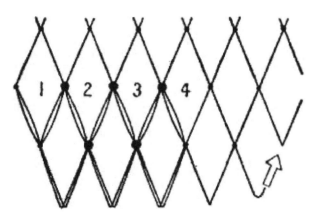

FIG. 51.

A double selvedge of this kind can be made without bating if the long-armed mesh is itself doubled over in the second doubling (Fig. 52) and the trebled twine is included in the next knot. The third part of the long arm then forms a small loop (Fig. 53) that can be picked up in the following round and no reduction in the number of meshes takes place.

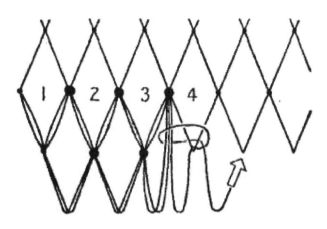

FIG. 52.

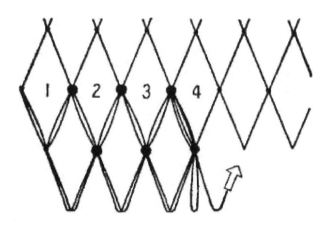

FIG. 53.

Doubling and Fly-meshing

There is yet another method of sloping a piece of net. It is called "doubling and fly-meshing" and the method is as follows:

On completion of a row double over the last mesh and then continue in the usual manner (Figs. 54 and 55). On return leave out the long-armed mesh, thus forming a special kind of fly-mesh. Return, and again double over the first mesh as before. The selvedge, when examined will then be found to consist of: long-armed mesh, bar of ordinary mesh, double mesh, and so on (Fig. 56).

FIG. 54.

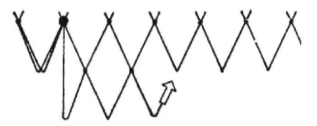

FIG. 55.

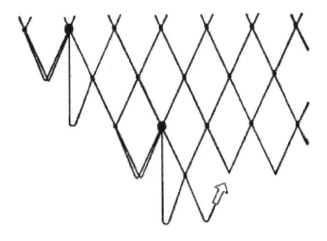

FIG. 56.

Creasing

The shape of a piece of net can be altered by increasing the number of meshes in successive rounds. This is generally known as "creasing." The commonest method of creasing is to make a small extra mesh beside the mesh just finished by making a second knot in the same place before picking up the next mesh (Fig. 57). In the next round this extra small mesh is picked up just as if it were an ordinary mesh, thus increasing the number of meshes (Fig. 58). It is usual to insert creasing meshes close to the selvedge it is desired to slope. If both selvedges are to be sloped a creasing mesh will be put in near the beginning and the end of each creasing round.

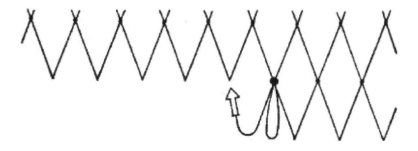

FIG. 57.

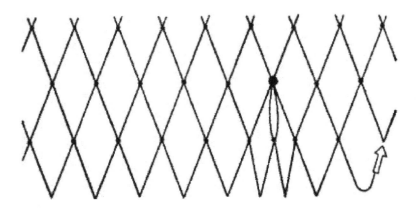

FIG. 58.

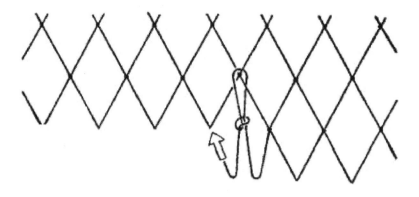

FIG. 59.

There is another method of putting in a creasing mesh that is often used in small-meshed nets where difficulty arises in pushing the needle through the small extra loop formed in the way already described. In this alternative method the needle is passed through the nearest half-mesh of the previous row but one. An overhand knot (Fig. 119, p. 82) is then made round the long arm so formed before picking up the next mesh in the ordinary way (Fig. 59). The small loop thus made is not locked as in an ordinary creasing, but is free to slide about and is therefore often known as a "slippery mesh." Fig. 60 shows what the creasing looks like when completed.

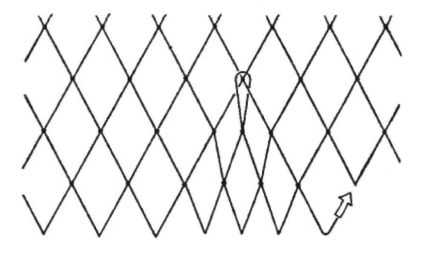

FIG. 60.

* Compare Fig. 23.

[1] i.e., abating or excepting.

CHAPTER III

SLEEVE NETS, BAG NETS AND SQUARE NETTING

NOT infrequently it is necessary to make a piece of netting in the shape of a cylinder or tube. This can be done by braiding an ordinary rectangular piece of net and joining together the opposite edges. In general, however, it is better for such nets to be "braided round." This can be done in several ways depending upon whether or not the tube is to be open at both ends (sleeve nets) or closed at one end so as to make a string bag or sack (bag nets).

Sleeve Netting—Method 1

Set up the net by method 1 for flat netting, working in the usual way from right to left. When the required number of half-meshes has been cast on, bring the starting and finishing end, S and F of the foundation line, together at positions S_1 and F_1—as indicated by the dotted lines in Fig. 61—and knot them firmly together to form a foundation loop, cutting off the superfluous ends if necessary (Fig. 62). Slip the ring of half-meshes so formed over a toggle suspended from a hook or a nail (Fig. 63). Now make the first mesh of the second round on the first mesh of the previous round as shown in the illustration, and carry on to complete round 2, sliding the foundation loop around the toggle as required. When the last mesh of this round is reached the long arm of the connecting mesh made at the beginning of the round should be included in the knot (Fig. 64). Carry on in this way, round upon round continuously in the same direction, until the required length has been reached. Then cut the foundation loop and release the first row of half-meshes. A piece of net made in this way will be cylindrical in shape. It can be narrowed or widened at one end by bating or creasing in the usual way.

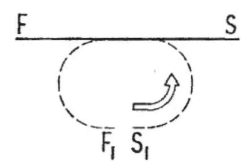

FIG. 61.

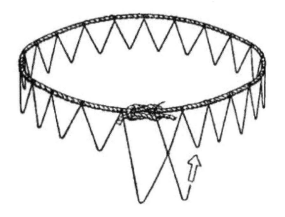

FIG. 62.

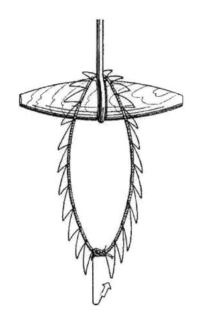

FIG. 63.

FIG. 64

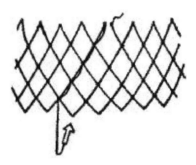

FIG. 65.

A joining line of doubled halvers[1] will be visible as shown in Fig. 65. Normally, this is no disadvantage except that "seamless" nets have perhaps a better appearance. These can be made by the method described below.

Sleeve Netting—Method 2

Make an independent loop of spare twine and hang it on a convenient hook. This is the foundation loop. Then unwind from the needle a length of twine a little longer than the length of the net it is intended to make. Allow this free length of twine—the standing part (Fig. 66S)—to hang down (to the floor if necessary) and grasp it with the left hand, nipping it firmly between the thumb and first finger. Pass the needle downwards through the foundation loop, in the direction *away* from you, bringing it forward again on the left of the standing part. Now draw the needle towards you until the distance between the foundation loop and the thumb of the left hand (which retains a non-slip grip of the standing part) is about equal to the length of one bar of the meshes it is desired to make. The working part (W) of the twine is now brought close to the standing part so that it too can be gripped between the finger and thumb of the left hand (Fig. 67). An overhand knot is then made around the standing part as shown in the figure. The distance from the foundation loop to the completed knot should equal the length of one side (bar) of the meshes of which the net will be made. If this distance is not quite right it can be adjusted by sliding the completed knot up or down a little bit on the standing part. The small loop so formed is a *setting-up* loop (S.L.1.) and is half the size of a full mesh.

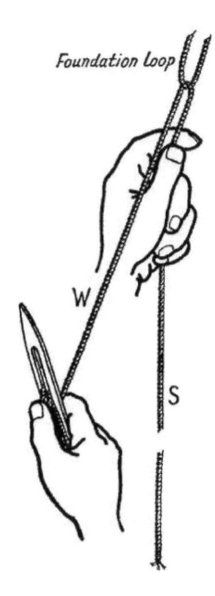

Foundation loop

W

S

FIG. 66.

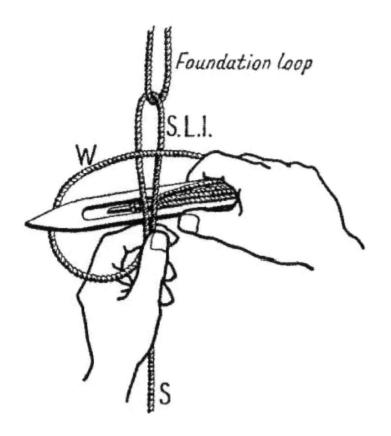

FIG. 67.

Now, using the fingers of the left hand as a gauge, as shown in Fig. 18 bend the twine around them, pass the needle once again away from you, down through the foundation loop, and then draw it back towards you until the knot already formed comes opposite the middle of the long side (L) of the large loop or *pseudo-mesh* (P) thus formed (Fig. 68). Then make another overhand knot on the long side (L) in the same way as before. When pulled tight this knot should be exactly level with the first one, and to the left of it. Continue in this way, working from right to left, until the number of setting-up loops is equal to the number of meshes required in the circumference of the net.

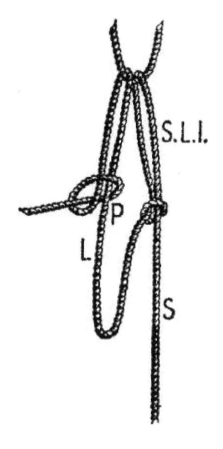

FIG. 68.

When this number is reached, grasp the standing part of the twine (i.e., the length of twine (S) hanging down from the knot of the first setting-up loop) between the first finger and thumb of the left hand and bring it side by side with the working part (W) of the twine (i.e., the part between the needle and the last knot). Now grasp both parts between finger and thumb and make an overhand knot, the *joining knot*, around the standing part in the usual way (Fig. 69).[1] When drawn tight this knot should be exactly level with the tips of the pseudo-meshes (Fig. 70). This done, use the appropriate gauge and continue braiding, round upon round from left to right, making on the standing part an overhand joining knot with the working part every time a round is completed. In this way a sleeve or cylinder of netting is made that has no obvious seam.

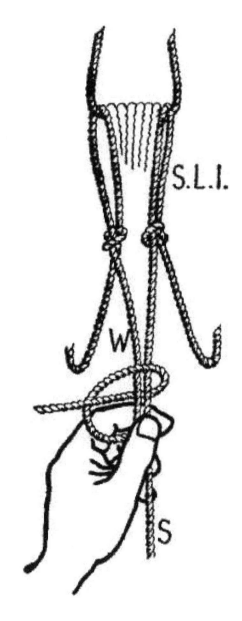

FIG. 69.

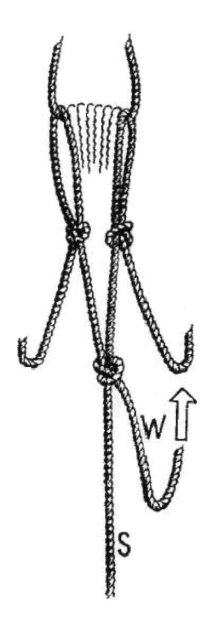

FIG. 70.

When the net is completed the foundation loop is removed and the setting-up loops are set free. This is the best method of making such things as the netting sleeves for net-ball goalposts. The setting-up loops can be made directly on the rings or they can be laced on after being set free from a foundation loop.

It will be noticed that the knots at the base of each setting-up loop, and the joining knots at the end of each round, are sliding knots. For most purposes there is no disadvantage in this. If however, properly locked knots are required, they can be used instead; they are made in the following way.

FIG. 71.

After passing the needle through the foundation loop as before, it is brought over towards the right so as to make the working part of the twine cross over the standing part (Fig. 71). Arrange the point of crossing so as to make the required size of foundation loop. Then nip both parts of the twine between the first finger and thumb of the left hand. Pass the needle from right to left through the loop so formed (Fig. 72) and then back again towards the right as indicated by the arrow ribbon. In this way a small closed loop or half-hitch is formed by the working part around the standing part hard up against the finger and thumb of the left hand (Fig. 73). Now pull strongly on the working part. This will cause the half-hitch to transfer itself from the working part to the standing part of the twine (Fig. 74). Now finish off the knot as if completing an ordinary sheet bend. The resulting non-slippery knot will appear as in Fig. 75. This knot may be used not only in making the setting-up loops but also at the end of every round when taking up the standing part in the joining knot.

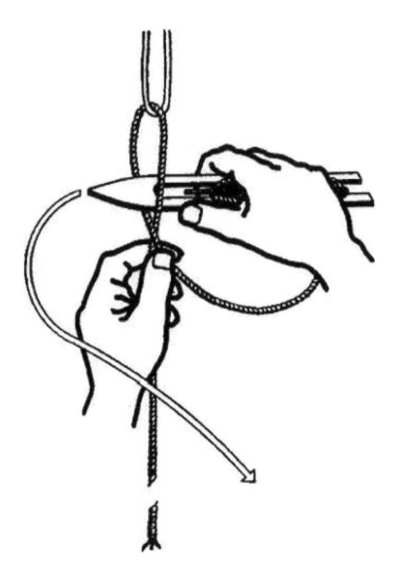

FIG. 72.

FIG. 73.

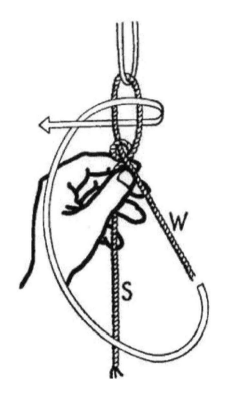

FIG. 74.

FIG. 75.

Bag Net—Method 1

A sleeve net may be closed at one end to make a string bag or sack. This can be done by lacing a line through the terminal meshes, drawing them tightly together, and knotting securely. This is rather a clumsy method.

Bag Net—Method 2

A better method than that described above is to make a sleeve net narrowed towards one end by bating until only a few meshes are left, and then take them all up in one final knot.

Bag Net—Method 3

The best method of making a bag net is to start from the closed end in the following manner. Unwind from a loaded needle a length of twine a little longer then the net to be made. Then form a simple bight and slip it over a convenient hook. With the working part now make an overhand knot around the standing part and adjust to form a large loop, the foundation loop.[1] Using this loop as if it were the half-mesh of a previous round, make another half-mesh on it, using the appropriate gauge as shown, passing the needle *upwards* through the foundation loop from the far side towards you (Fig. 76). The knot is completed in the normal manner (Fig. 77). Continue in this way forming a series of loops around the gauge and a row of foundation knots along its upper edge (Fig. 78). When the required number of loops has been made— i.e., the number of meshes needed for the net—remove the gauge and lift the foundation loop off its hook. Then pass the standing part through the eye of the foundation loop. This done, grasp the standing part at the point S (Fig. 79) and with a strong pull draw it through the knots until the eye of the foundation loop is tightly closed around the standing end (Fig. 80). Now grasp the standing end at ST and draw it through the closed eye. This will cause the row of knots to bend into a ring, pressing the first-formed knot firmly up against the last-formed one (Fig. 81), and bringing the working part (W) of the twine side by side with the standing part (S). Now prepare a toggle by tying one end of a piece of strong string to an ordinary overall button (Fig. 82). Pass the toggle-line through the small hole formed in the centre of the ring of knots and suspend the whole from a hook (Fig. 81). Be sure that the working part of the twine is on the left of the standing part. If the toggle-string is passed through the knots in the wrong direction the working and standing parts will be reversed. If this happens the toggle-string must be removed and passed through the hole from the other side. This will bring the two parts of the twine into the correct position. This done, they should be knotted firmly together with a reef knot formed hard up against the foundation knots where the two parts emerge from them.

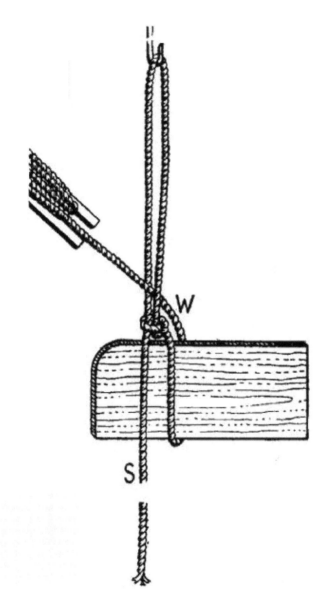

FIG. 76.

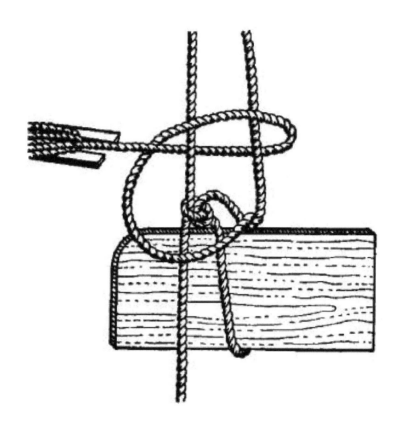

FIG. 77.

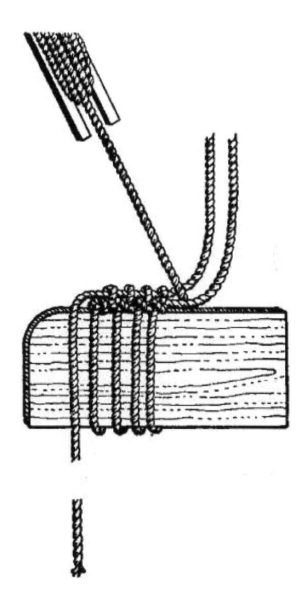

FIG. 78.

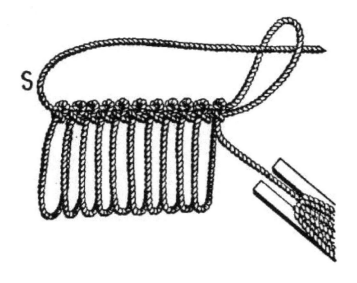

FIG. 79.

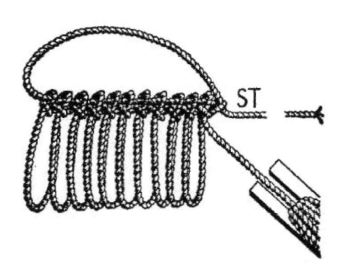

FIG. 80.

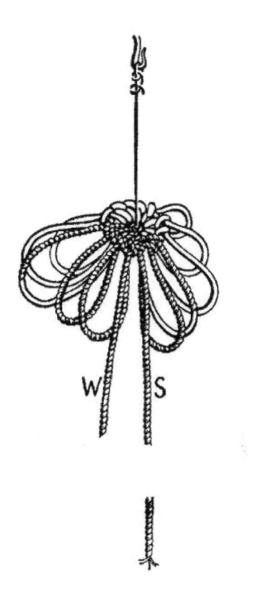

FIG. 81.

FIG. 82.

Round 2 is now commenced on the first ring of half-meshes, not forgetting first of all to make a joining knot on the standing part as described under method 2 for sleeve netting. Continue in this way, round upon round, until the desired size is reached. By this method, string bags, dip nets and such like can be made quickly and accurately, the original ring of knots making a very pretty pattern at the bottom. The nets can be further shaped by appropriate creasing and bating, or by varying the size of the meshes.

Square Netting

In all ordinary pieces of flat, sleeve and bag netting, the meshes hang diamond-wise. But in certain nets, such as tennis nets and the "armouring" of some trammel nets, the meshes "hang square." In netting made in the ordinary way the meshes cannot satisfactorily be made to hang square no matter how they are mounted on the supporting ropes or wires. If a net is required to hang square it must be specially made for the purpose. The actual knots and meshes are made in exactly the same way as in ordinary diamond netting and the proper "hang" is given by an ingenious series of batings and creasings. The method is as follows:

Commence with one mesh (as in chaining out) hung from an appropriate hook (Fig. 83). On it make another mesh (2), working as usual from left to right. Then make a creasing mesh (3) before beginning the next round, right to left (Fig. 84). On reaching the left selvedge again (with mesh 5) make another creasing mesh (6) before turning back on the next round, left to right again (Fig. 85). In this way, making a creasing mesh on each selvedge before beginning the following round, continue until the necessary *depth* of the net is reached on selvedge *A* (mesh 45 in Fig. 86). When this occurs, make one more row as before, crease again on the far selvedge (*B*), and return to *A*. But when the selvedge at *A* is reached this time, make a bating by picking up meshes 46 and 47 together in one knot when making mesh 64. Continue thus, creasing and bating in alternate rounds on opposite selvedges, until the required *length* of net is reached along selvedge *B*. Then finish off by *bating* on both selvedges until, finally, only one mesh remains.

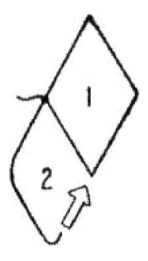

FIG. 83.

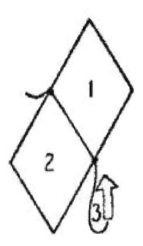

FIG. 84.

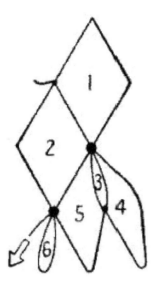

FIG. 85.

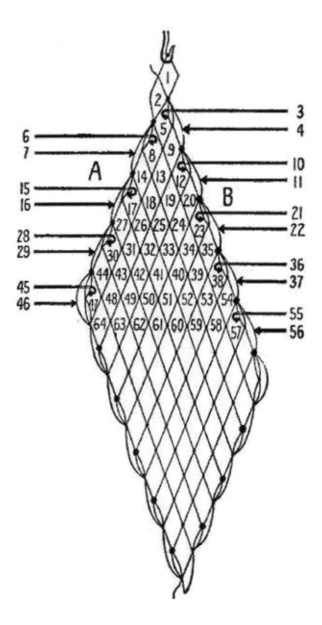

FIG. 86.

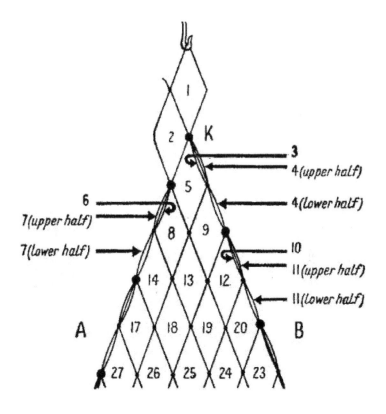

FIG. 87.

Normal selvedges are shown in Fig. 86. A stronger margin and neater appearance are obtained by making straight selvedges in the usual way—i.e., by including in its own knot the long arm of the first mesh in each row. The result will appear as in Fig. 87 with triple twine and double twine alternating along both selvedges and at the head and foot of the net. In practice the long arm of mesh 2 would have been included in its own knot at K but this has not been done in Fig. 87. When the net is finished the original knot is untied and the first-formed mesh disappears. In use, the net is taped and mounted along selvedge *B* which will form the upper edge of the net.[1] The meshes will then become perfectly symmetrical squares as illustrated in Fig. 88.

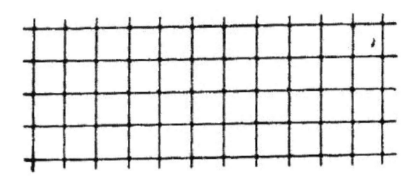

FIG. 88.

[1] *Vide* p. 70 and Fig. 104.

[1] In this and the following figure the first and last setting-up loops only are fully shown for the sake of clarity.

[1] Note carefully that in this method the foundation loop is not made from a separate piece of twine that will later be discarded.

[1] *Vide* Fig. 162 on p. 108.

CHAPTER IV

HOW TO MOUNT A NET

MOST pieces of netting, before use, must be affixed to some kind of line or rope around some or all of their edges. This is described as "mounting" or "fixing" a net. Various ways of doing this will now be described.

The meshes of ordinary netting hang diamond-wise as in Fig. 39. The shape of the diamonds can be varied by the way the meshes are spread out on the rope at the head of the net— i.e., on the "headline." The closer the meshes are spaced on the headline, the narrower and deeper the meshes will be. It is necessary to give names to these various degrees of closeness and openness. For example, a favourite mounting is to make three meshes occupy the space of two fully stretched ones as in Fig. 89; that is to say, if the mesh bars of this net were 2 in. long, the distance between *A* and *B*, three meshes apart on the headline, would be 8 in.—which is the length of four bars or two fully stretched meshes. This mounting is known as "setting in by the third." If it is necessary to have the net pulled out more widely four meshes can be made to occupy the space of three, five the space of four, and so on. This would be termed "setting in by the fourth" and "setting in by the fifth" respectively. If the meshes must be more elongated vertically, and therefore narrower, two meshes can be made to occupy the space of one. This is "setting in by the half" (Fig. 90). When more than three but less than four meshes (e.g., $3\frac{1}{2}$ meshes) occupy the space of two the setting is "without the third" (Fig. 91). If more than two but less than three meshes (e.g., $2\frac{1}{2}$ meshes) were to occupy the space of two the setting would be "within the third" and so on. When the meshes at the foot of a net are also mounted on a "footrope" the spacing must be the same as on the headline.

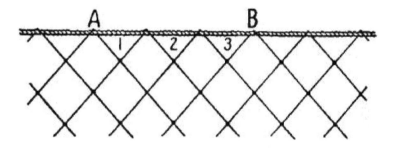

FIG. 89.

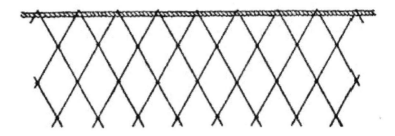

FIG. 90.

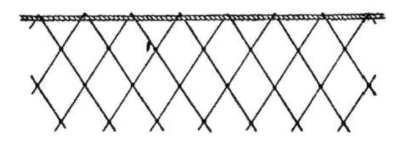

FIG. 91.

Reeving

A single sheet of netting suspended from a rope along its upper edge is known as a piece of "wall netting." There are various ways of setting an ordinary wall net on its headline. Let us assume that a 60-yd. length of netting has to be set in by the third. The easiest and quickest—but least satisfactory—way to do this is simply to reeve a line through the head meshes and fix the end ones at points 40 yds. apart. The intervening meshes are then spread evenly along the line and every sixth, twelfth, or twentieth mesh (as the case may be) is hitched securely in position.

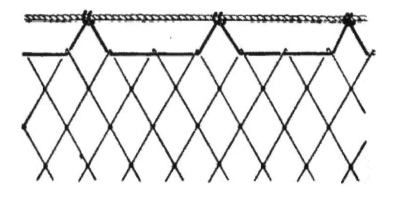

FIG. 92.

Stapling

A second and better method is that known as "stapling." Let us assume that in our net the meshes are of 2-in. bar, and that it is to be set in by the half. A light stapling line is hitched securely to the headline near one end. The free end of the stapling line is then rove through the first three head meshes of the net and hitched again to the headline at a point 6 in. from the first knot, leaving a little slack to form a bight or staple (Fig. 92). Repeat until all the head meshes have been taken up in this way, the distance between any two adjacent knots being 6 in. Longer staples, taking up more than three meshes may at times be used with advantage.

Norselling

A third method is known as "osselling" or "norselling." Reeve a light line through the head meshes as in method 1. Then at every sixth mesh (or thereabout) attach a short piece of line a foot or so long which is then carried up and attached by its other end to the main headline (Fig. 93). These short lengths of line are the "ossels" or "norsels." The knot (*A*) made on the main headline is a special one known as the ossel knot. The knot (*B*) made at the other end of the ossel is an ossel hitch (*vide* Figs. 133 and 134).

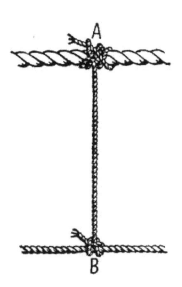

FIG. 93.

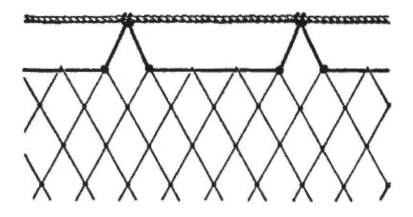

FIG. 94.

Norselling and Stapling

In yet another method the stapling line is knotted to the end meshes of each staple (Fig. 94). The result amounts to what is, in effect, a combination of osselling and stapling. In special cases the head and foot meshes are attached direct to the mounting ropes by means of clove hitches as the net is being made.

Hitchings

Selvedges are usually attached to their mounting ropes by marline hitchings. If an ordinary selvedge has been formed each mesh will be taken up in its own hitch (Fig. 95). In straight selvedges, the hitchings will be evenly spaced along the ropes, hard up against the selvedge knots of the net.

To do this, the rope on which the net is to be mounted is stretched tightly between two supports. Take up a position on the right-hand side of this rope with the net stretched along the ground on the other side. Begin at one end; either end will do according to whether you prefer to work backwards or forwards. Let us assume that you decide to work forwards. With a loaded needle make a clove hitch on the mounting rope and one or two additional hitches beside it for extra strength. Pick up the end of the net and include the corner mesh in the final hitches. Now carry the marling line forward with the left hand and make a loop where the next hitch is to be formed (Fig. 96). Pass the needle under the rope, through the net[1] and up through the loop. Pull tight and a marline hitch will be formed. Be sure the loop in the marling line is formed correctly or a proper marline hitch will not be formed. Compare the loop in Fig. 96, *which is correct*, with that in Fig. 97, *which is incorrect*.

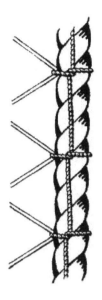

FIG. 95.

FIG. 96.

FIG. 97.

FIG. 98.

FIG. 99.

Simple half-hitchings are sometimes used in place of marline hitchings. These are formed by passing the needle around the mounting rope and up under the marling line without first making a loop (Fig. 98). They are not nearly so secure as marline hitchings.

FIG. 100.

Some workers prefer to work backwards. The methods are the same, the details only being different. Fig. 99 shows the formation of a marline hitch when working in this direction. It can also be formed as shown in Fig. 100. The formation of a simple half-hitching is shown in Fig. 101. It is usual, at frequent intervals, to make an extra hitch alongside the ordinary hitchings to prevent the whole thing coming adrift if a break occurs anywhere in the marling line. This is particularly necessary if simple half-hitchings are used.

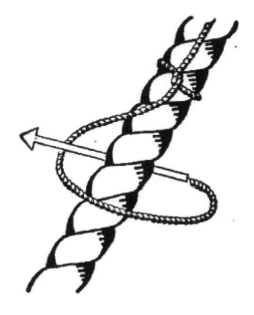

FIG. 101.

Stapling Fly Meshes

Where the selvedge consists of a series of fly-meshes (as in the wings of some trawls) a special kind of stapling is used. One end of the stapling line is knotted firmly on the rope. This line is then passed through one corner of the nearest fly-mesh and then through the adjacent corner of the next fly-mesh after which the next knot is tied. Each fly-mesh is thus included in two staples and each staple takes in two fly-meshes (Fig. 102).[1] By this method a great deal of "give" is provided in the selvedge which for certain purposes, as in the wings of trawls, may be an advantage. Normally, the width of each staple should be roughly equal to two bars of the net; in other words, adjacent stapling knots should be separated by the distance between three knots in the net.

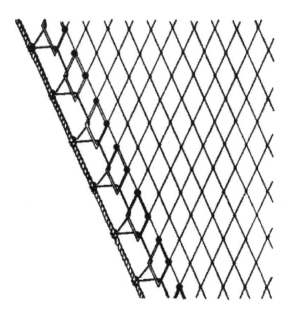

FIG. 102.

[1] In Figs. 96–101 the net is not shown.

[1] Note the doubled fly-meshes.

CHAPTER V

HOW TO MEND

General Principles

For most people, the art of mending holes in nets is more difficult to master than the art of making them. But with a little practice, aided by the judicious use of pencil and paper, the difficulties can soon be overcome.

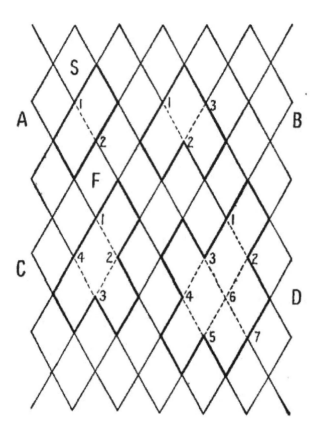

FIG. 103.

Let us start with the simplest hole caused by breaking a single mesh bar, as indicated by the broken line opposite *A* in Fig. 103. Though simple, this break is extremely important because each of the two long sides of the resulting hole (outlined in heavy lines) consists of a straight line, the length of two mesh bars, with a knot in the middle of it. A straight side of this kind, two bars in length, is called a "halver."

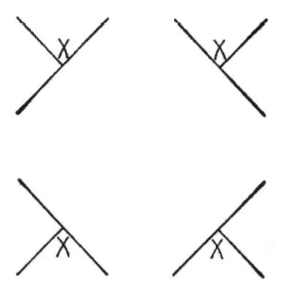

FIG. 104.

Examination of any piece of netting (or a simple sketch) will reveal that four kinds of halvers are possible, depending on the position of the broken bar or bars. These four types of halver are illustrated in Fig. 104. They are left-hand and right-hand upper halvers, and left-hand and right-hand lower halvers. Depending upon the size and type of hole, mending can start and finish on any kind of halver at its middle point (X). In upper halvers, this point is really the lower tip of an undamaged mesh, and in lower halvers it is the upper tip of an undamaged mesh. This will be clear by a closer study of Fig. 103.

All holes, big or small, must contain two halvers *and not more than two.* Any hole containing more than two halvers cannot be mended without doubling over some bars of one or more meshes. In a correctly-mended hole doubling is not permissible. Before starting any mend, therefore, examine the hole and cut around its edges in such a way as to leave one convenient halver to start on and one to finish on. If the hole consists of more than a very few broken bars, the starting halver will be at the top of the hole and the finishing halver at the bottom.

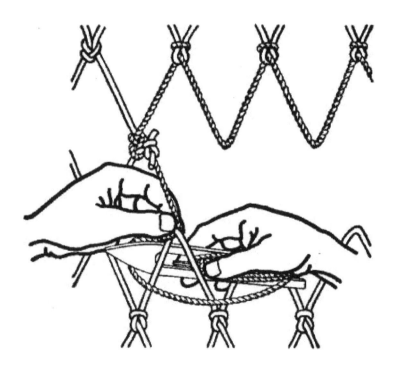

FIG. 105.

In the simplest hole, formed by one broken bar, no "cutting out" is necessary as two halvers are automatically formed, and no more (Fig. 103A). This hole would be mended by starting in the middle of the upper halver—that is to say, by picking up the bottom tip of the mesh marked S in the figure, and forming on it an ordinary netting knot. This is done by bringing the needle up through S from the far side towards you and then completing on it a sheet bend in the usual way (Fig. 22). The upper tip of mesh F is then picked up by passing the needle *down* through it from the far side towards you and completing the sheet bend as shown in Fig. 105.[1] Before this knot is formed the new mesh bar (Fig. 103A—dotted line) must be adjusted to the correct length. The figures 1 and 2 in this hole indicate the first and second (which is also the last) knots in this mend.

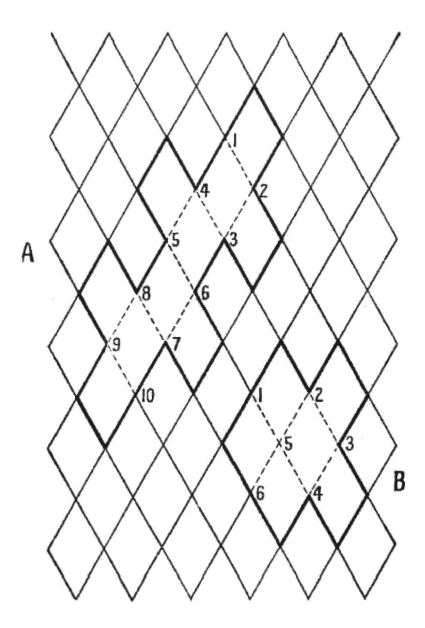

FIG. 106.

A slightly bigger hole is illustrated opposite *B* in Fig. 103. Here two mesh bars have been broken but again no cutting out is necessary as only two halvers have been formed. To mend this hole commence at 1, pick up the bottom mesh at 2 as shown in Fig. 105 and finish at 3. Points 1 and 3 are the midpoints of two halvers. Other holes all ready for mending are shown in Figs. 103C and D, and in Figs. 106A and B. The numbering shows where the successive knots are to be made, and the dotted lines indicate the new twine with which the holes are mended.[1]

In mending a more complicated hole such as is shown at Fig. 103D it will be found that, in addition to the halvers at points 1 and 7, where the mend begins and ends, a right-hand side-mesh has to be picked up at 2, an ordinary upper mesh at 3, a left-hand side-mesh at 4, a bottom mesh at 5 and an upper mesh again at 6. We already know how to take up an upper mesh when braiding in the direction right to left. This must be remembered at 3 or a twisted mesh will result. Taking up the mesh for knot 6 is done by the simple left-to-right method. But picking up the side knots involves new procedures that must now be described.

Side Mesh—Right-hand Side of Hole

Pick up the free knot of the side mesh between the first finger and thumb of the left hand and bring the working part of the mending twine down alongside it on the outside of the mesh—i.e., on the left of the knot (Fig. 107). Then pass the needle down through the mesh and out again around the left-hand lower bar as indicated by the arrow ribbon. Draw tightly and a half-hitch will be formed by the mending twine around the mesh bar close up to the knot (Fig. 108). Grasp firmly between the first finger and thumb in order to prevent slackening, and complete the knot as in making an ordinary sheet bend. This will produce the knot shown in Fig. 109. Some menders consider that a better lead to the next mesh is obtained by passing the needle in the opposite direction when completing the knot (Fig. 110). The result is then as shown in Fig. 111.[1]

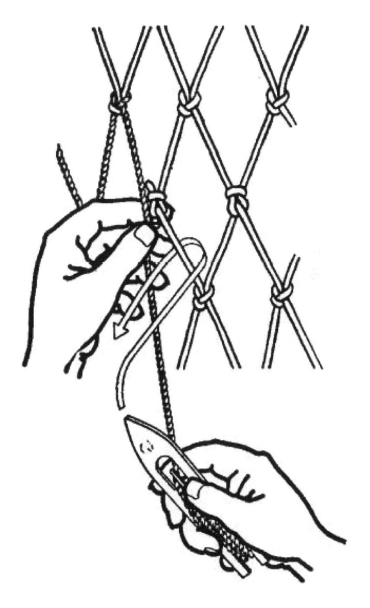

FIG. 107.

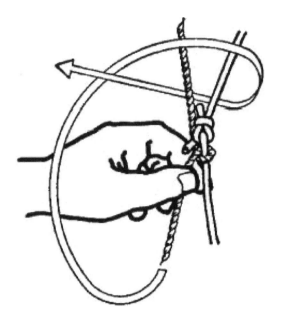

FIG. 108.

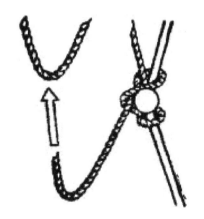

FIG. 109.

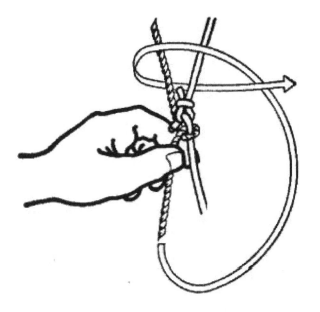

FIG. 110.

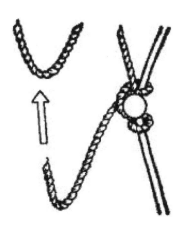

FIG. 111.

Side Mesh—Left-hand Side of Hole

Again pick up the free knot of the side mesh between the first finger and thumb of the left hand. Then lay the working part of the mending twine alongside this knot on the side next the mesh opening, i.e., on the left of the knot (Fig. 112). Next pass the needle under and over the lower bar of the side-mesh as indicated by the arrow ribbon. Draw tightly, and a half-hitch will be formed by the mending twine around the mesh bar, below and close up against the knot (Fig. 113). Complete in the usual way. The side mesh as "taken up" will appear as in Fig. 114.

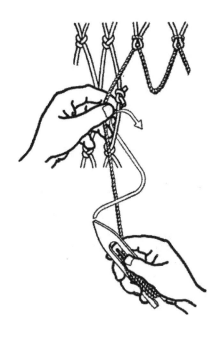

FIG. 112.

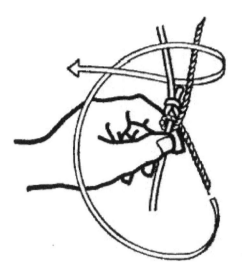

FIG. 113.

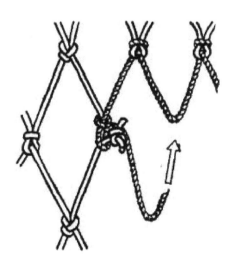

FIG. 114.

Quick Method

When a hole has to be mended in the shortest possible time, a side mesh can be taken up merely by including its knot in an ordinary overhand knot formed on the mending twine. The fingering for doing this on the right-hand side is shown in Fig. 115 and on the left-hand side in Fig. 116.

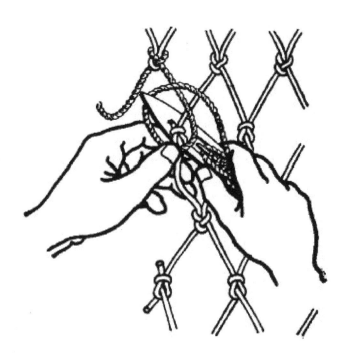

FIG. 115.

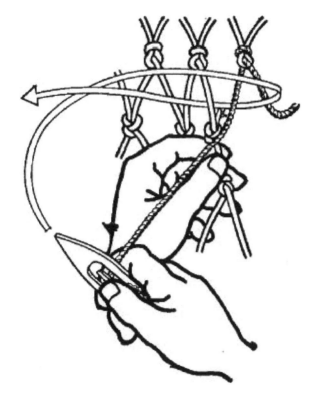

FIG. 116.

Large Mend—fully described

Having got thus far the learner should now be able to cope with the holes shown in Figs. 103C and D, and in Figs. 106A and B, particular attention being given to recognising the halvers on which the mends are begun and ended. Finally, a large hole is shown in Fig. 117, the thin lines indicating its appearance before cutting out. The thick line shows how the cutting out should be done with the least possible loss of undamaged net. The same hole, duly mended, is shown in Fig. 118, the numbers again showing the sequence in which the knots would be made. In all these diagrams the numbers are on the right of the knots to which they refer.

Beginners should study the following analysis carefully until it is fully understood and the various features easily recognisable in any hole in a piece of actual net.

Mending commences at 1 (Fig. 118) on a right-hand upper halver at the top of the hole. From here braid towards the left making knots 2–5 as if making an ordinary piece of new net (using a gauge if necessary to get the meshes even) until knot 5 is reached. Knot 6 takes up a left-hand side-mesh. Next braid towards the right making knots 7–10. Knot 11 takes up a right-hand side-mesh. Now ordinary braiding again, making knots 12–17 in the ordinary right-to-left manner. Notice that with knots 12–15 newly-made meshes have been taken up. With knots 16 and 17, meshes of the original net are taken up. From 17 proceed to take up a side mesh with knot 18 and then a bottom mesh at knot 19 before making the next ordinary left-to-right row of knots 20–26. From now on, a side mesh and a bottom mesh are taken up on each side (before commencing the next row across the hole) until the left-hand side-mesh is taken up at knot 48. From here there is no bottom mesh waiting to be taken up so the next round is begun normally at knot 49. Beyond this point no new features are encountered until knot 67 is completed. With knot 68 a bottom mesh is taken up, knot 69 is normal, back again to a bottom mesh at knot 70—and so on until knot 77 is made. Now everything is straightforward again until side-knot 80 is made. Knot 81 picks up a bottom mesh; knot 82 is normal; 83 picks up a bottom mesh; 84 is normal; knot 85 picks up a left-hand side-mesh and 86 is the finishing knot made on a right-hand bottom halver.

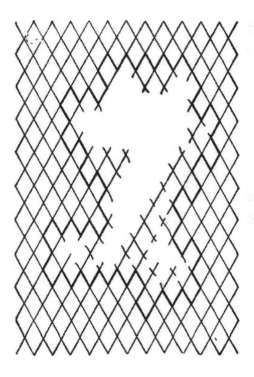

FIG. 117.

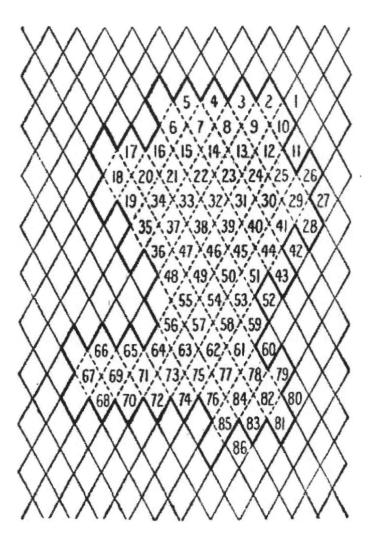

FIG. 118.

It is highly important, in mending, to remember to pass the needle correctly through all upper meshes when braiding from right to left, and left to right. When taking up bottom meshes, the needle should always be passed down through them from the far side towards you. If a bottom mesh is taken up when working from left to right, the knot is completed by passing the needle behind the mesh bars and through the bight of the twine, *from right to left* as shown in Fig. 105. If a bottom mesh is taken up when going from right to left the bight of the twine is thrown to the right and the needle passed behind the mesh bars *from left to right*. If the needle is passed in the wrong direction behind the mesh bars when completing the knots, the mending twine will lead in the wrong direction when it emerges from the finished knot, and "twisted meshes" will result. In mending it is also important to remember that the free knots in the top and bottom meshes can be unpicked and the bits of waste twine discarded. Side knots cannot be unpicked; if this is done the mesh bars come apart and the mesh is destroyed.

[1] N.B. This figure depicts a bigger hole than is formed by a single broken bar.

[1] The beginner, when learning how to mend, will find it helpful to use mending twine of a different colour from that of the net.

[1] In Figs. 109 and 111 the detail of the original side knot is omitted for the sake of clarity.

CHAPTER VI

ESSENTIAL KNOTS AND HITCHES

IN net-making certain knots and hitches, in addition to the sheet bend, must be used. It is necessary, therefore, to include descriptions of them in this book.[1]

The Overhand Knot

The simplest of all knots is the overhand or thumb knot. It is universally used for finishing off loose ends to prevent the strands from unlaying. It is illustrated in Fig. 119 and its construction is obvious.

_end

FIG. 119.

The Interlaced Overhand Knot

This is a very useful knot often used for joining two pieces of twine as, for example, when starting with a fresh needle during braiding. Make an overhand knot on the old end. Then pass the free end of the fresh twine through the knot alongside the free end of the old twine and follow around as shown by the arrow ribbon in Fig. 120. This makes a very secure join and at the same time gives a direct lead through it—a very great virtue in any joining knot.[1] Fig. 121 shows the knot drawn tight. It is very difficult to untie, especially after it has been wetted.

FIG. 120.

135

FIG. 121.

FIG. 122.

The Double Overhand Knot

The knot described above is often wrongly named the double overhand knot. The true knot of this name is formed by laying two pieces of twine side by side and making an overhand knot on both of them; in other words it is simply an overhand knot made with double twine (Fig. 122). It should never be used as a joining knot.

The Fisherman's Knot

This, or the interlaced overhand knot described above, should always be used when joining together two lengths of twine in net-making. With the free end of each piece of twine tie a compact overhand knot round the other piece. Be sure that the ends are correctly led (Fig. 123) or the knot will not form properly. Fig. 124 shows the ends incorrectly led through. Draw the two parts together and pull tight The two knots will twist round slightly so as to fit snugly together (Fig. 125) and the finished knot will appear as in Fig. 126. This knot is extremely secure but can easily be untied by gripping the free ends and drawing the component knots apart again. Then each can be untied without difficulty.

FIG. 123.

FIG. 124.

FIG. 125.

FIG. 126.

The Bowline

This is an invaluable knot that should always be used for making a non-slip loop on the end of twine or rope. Make a loop, as shown in Fig. 127, and grip the point of crossing-over between the first finger and thumb of the right hand, with the thumb underneath. Then, without changing the grip with either hand, make a clockwise twist with the right hand as indicated by the arrow ribbon. This will produce a small loop on the standing part of the twine with the free end coming up inside it (Fig. 128). Now transfer the grip of the left hand to this loop where the twine crosses over (Fig. 128A) and hold both parts firmly in position so that the loops keep their size and shape. Then, with the right hand, complete the knot by leading the free end behind the standing part and down through the small loop as shown by the arrow ribbon. The finished knot will appear as in Fig. 129. Pull tight.

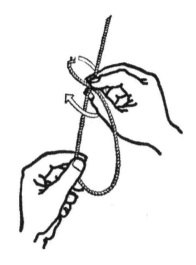

FIG. 127.

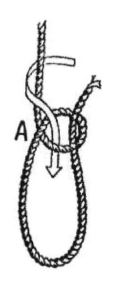

FIG. 128.

FIG. 129.

The Reef Knot

This is a useful knot for uniting the ends of ropes or twines of the same size and consistency. But because of the ease with which it can be made it is all too frequently used as a joining knot when these conditions are not fulfilled. It is then almost useless for it easily slips and comes adrift. It should never be used for joining the twine in net-making.

FIG. 130.

FIG. 131.

FIG. 132.

To form the knot take an end in each hand and lay one over the other as shown in Fig. 130. Then take the free end nearest the right hand and lead it as indicated by the arrow ribbon. Pull tight and the completed knot will appear as in Fig. 131. It is easily untied by pulling one of the free ends back towards the other free end.

If the ends are led incorrectly a false reef or granny knot is formed (Fig. 132), which "should never be used for any purpose whatsoever."[1]

The Ossel Knot

When mounting nets by the osselling method, the ossel knot (Fig. 133) is used on the larger of the two ropes. Hold the ossel near one end and let it hang down on the side of the rope next you. Then with the upper end of the ossel make a complete turn around the rope, over the left thumb at T, and over its own part at P. Make a second turn, missing the thumb this time, but again including its own part. A third turn is now made on the right of the standing part and the end carried back across all three turns and under at T. Remove the thumb and work tight. This knot will not slip along the rope or become undone. For this reason it is also used for attaching snoods to fishing lines. The completed knot drawn tight is shown in Fig. 93A.

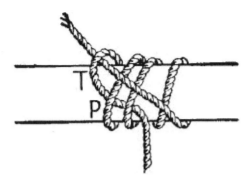

FIG. 133.

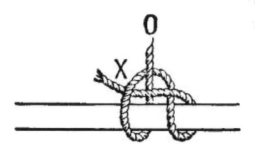

FIG. 134.

The Ossel Hitch

The lower end of the ossel is attached to the lighter line with an ossel hitch (Fig. 134). Bring the end down past the line on the side away from you and carry it up in front, on the left of the standing part (O). Then pass it towards the right behind 0, down in front of the line and up behind it, then to

145

the left, over its own part and in front of O, then under at X. Pull tight. The completed hitch drawn tight is shown in Fig. 93B.

In certain types of nets, such as herring, pilchard and mackerel drift nets, specially made ossels are used which have a loop at one end (Fig. 135). With these ossels the ossel hitch is not used. Instead a lark's head knot (Fig. 136) is formed by passing the standing part of the ossel around the line and through its own loop. The ordinary ossel knot is made at the other end.

FIG. 135.

FIG. 136.

The Flat Knot

Often, in small-meshed nets, reef knots are used for making the meshes instead of the usual sheet bend. These reef knots, technically known to net-makers as "flat knots," are quite as easily made as the more usual ones. The needle is passed through the loop of the half-mesh of the previous round in the direction away from you, then towards the left, and out behind the left-hand bar of the half-mesh (Fig. 137). In the second movement the needle is passed behind the right-hand bar only of the half-mesh, then towards you and out through the opening of the loop (Fig. 138).[1] The finished knot is shown in the inset to this figure. There is no change in the method of passing the needle when working from right to left. Braiding with the flat knot differs therefore in this respect from the sheet bend method.

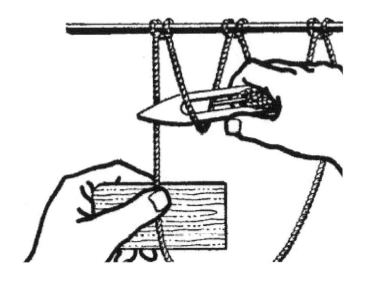

FIG. 137.

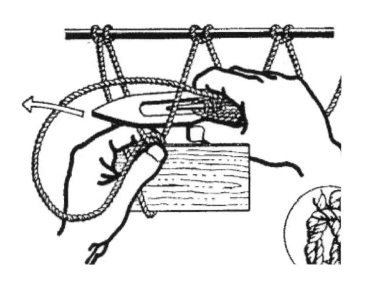

FIG. 138.

The "Martha's Vineyard" Netting Knot

This is the normal knot for filet work but is also used in net-making so must be described here. It closely resembles the normal sheet bend but differs from it in the way the parts cross over one another, as will be seen on comparing the inset to Fig. 139 with Figs. 26 and 27. It is not an easy knot to learn but when mastered high speeds can be attained. Certain West African native fishermen habitually use this knot when braiding beach seines.

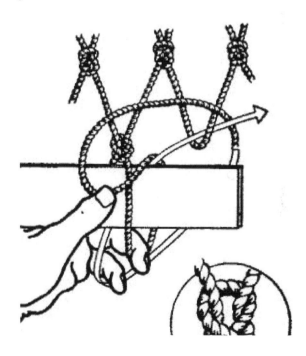

FIG. 139.

A long gauge is needed and the grip is shown in Fig. 139. Bring the twine down, as usual, on the side of the gauge next you and over the fourth finger of the left hand, up the far side and over the top until it can be gripped by the left thumb. Now go down again on the far side, over the little finger, up through the loop round the gauge, through the half-mesh of the previous round and then over to the right through the working loop. The whole process is clearly shown in the figure.

Now pull firmly downwards, releasing as you do so, first the loop on the fourth finger, then the loop on the little finger, and a knot, as illustrated, will be formed. It is easier to pass the needle through the previous half-mesh in the direction opposite to that shown in the figure—i.e., from the far side towards you—but if that is done a twisted mesh results. This is of no importance if very fine twine or thread is being used but for nets of stouter material twisted meshes should be avoided. This knot can be worked only in the left-to-right direction so setting up should be done on a foundation loop, or on a foundation line that can be worked from *both* sides, or by chaining out.

[1] For detailed descriptions and figures of other useful knots see *Knots, Ties and Splices* by Burgess and Irving. Rontledge & Kegan Paul Ltd. Price 3/6.

[1] Compare this knot with that shown in Fig. 126, which does *not* give a direct lead through it.

[1] See *Knots, Ties and Splices*, p. 34. By Burgess and Irving. Routledge & Kegan Paul Ltd.

[1] Figs. 137 and 138 should be compared with Figs. 20–23 which show the formation of the normal sheet bend netting knot.

CHAPTER VII

SOME THINGS TO MAKE

UP to this point this book has been concerned mainly with providing practice in making pieces of net of different shapes and sizes, attaching them to mounting ropes, and with mending holes in torn netting. The learner who has worked carefully through the previous pages should therefore now be able to follow the directions given in this chapter for making a representative series of useful articles. The selection is by no means exhaustive; it is merely a sound and suggestive basis for unlimited extension. Anyone who can make string bags will be able to make anglers' keep and landing nets; the square "armouring" of trammel nets is made in exactly the same way as a tennis netting; football goal nets, cricket nets, boundary nets and garden nets of all kinds consist either of simple rectangular pieces of flat netting or of sections of flat netting suitably shaped and joined together; and even fishing nets, in all their multiplicity of shapes and sizes, consist of flat netting, sleeve netting, or bag netting, or skilful combinations of them. Full and detailed descriptions of how to make the many kinds of fishing nets[1] used in this country alone would fill many volumes; but a thorough understanding of any of them can easily be built upon a good grasp of the basic principles of net braiding all of which are required in making the articles described in the following pages.

String Bag for Tennis Balls

Set up by method 3 for bag nets as described. Use size 6 cotton twine.

FIG. 140.

i. Cast on 12 setting-up loops (round 1)—$1\frac{1}{2}$ in. bar.

ii. Make a closed ring as described and suspend on a toggle.

iii. Make 7 more rounds (2–8).

iv. Make 1 round (9), double twine, to finish.

v. Lace a thick cord, about 20 in. long, through the last (doubled) row and splice the ends neatly together. This is the closing and carrying cord. A piece of good quality hemp (size 10) is best for this purpose as it can be spliced easily and neatly. The finished bag will appear as in Fig. 140.

Simple string bags of all sizes can be made in this way by varying the number and size of the meshes. A large bag for carrying a football is described below.

Note carefully the difference between *lacing* a line through meshes and *reeving* a line through them. In Fig. 141 the line is *laced* through the top meshes, the bars of which are seen to be *over* and *under* alternately as they are followed along the length of the line. In Fig. 142 the line is *rove* through the top meshes, the bars of which are seen to be *over, over* and *under, under* as they are traced along.

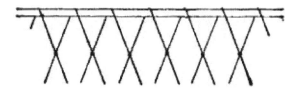

FIG. 141.

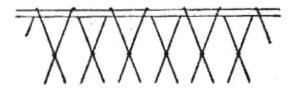

FIG. 142.

Carrying Net for a Football

Set up by method 3 for bag nets. Use size 6 or 7 cotton twine.

i. Cast on 18 setting-up loops (round 1)—$1\frac{1}{2}$ in. bar.

ii. Make a closed ring and suspend on a toggle.

iii. Make 3 ordinary rounds (2–4).

iv. Make 1 bating in each of the next 5 rounds (5–9).

v. Make 1 ordinary round (10).

vi. Make 1 round with double twine to finish (11).

155

This will produce a string bag 11 rounds deep (i.e., 10 rounds plus the setting-up round) and having 13 (i.e., 18–5) meshes around the mouth.

Lace a stout cord about 2 ft. 9 in, long, preferably good quality hemp, size 10 or 11, through the last (doubled) round and splice the ends neatly together.

Double-ended Carrying Bag for Bowls

The completed bag will appear as in Fig. 143. There is an opening in the side through which the bowls are put in and taken out, the bag being closed at both ends. One bowl (or "wood") reposes in each end and the bag is carried by the middle (Fig. 144).

FIG. 143.

FIG. 144.

Set up by method 3 for bag nets . Use size 6 or 7 cotton twine.

i. Cast on 12 setting-up loops (round 1)—$1\frac{3}{4}$ in. bar.

ii. Make a closed ring and suspend on a toggle.

iii. Make 5 complete rounds.

iv. At the end of the 6th round omit the joining knot on the standing part and make a return round (7)—right-to-left—as if braiding a normal piece of flat netting (Fig. 145). Make a straight selvedge (see Fig. 40). At the end of this round include the standing part in the selvedge knot (Figs. 146 and 147).

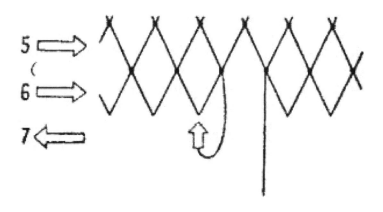

FIG. 145.

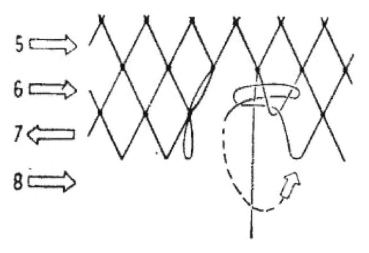

FIG. 146.

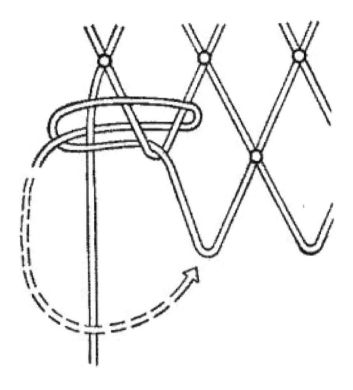

FIG. 147.

v. Make 2 more rounds (8 and 9)—left-to-right and right-to-left—continuing to omit the joining knot. Make straight selvedges on both sides of the opening and include the standing part in all selvedge knots on its own side (Fig. 148).

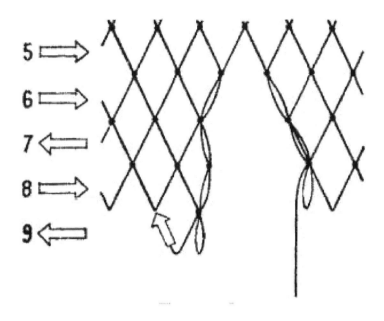

FIG. 148.

vi. Make round 10. When the selvedge is reached at the end of this round make a joining knot on the standing part to close the opening and continue braiding towards the right in the usual circular manner (Fig. 149).

vii. Make 5 more rounds (11–15)—circular braiding.

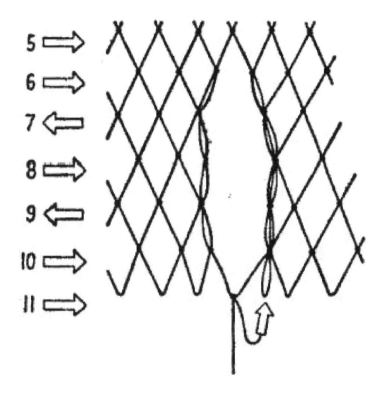

FIG. 149.

viii. Finish by making a final round of knots hard up against one another without any loops (half-meshes) between them (Fig. 150). This closes the end and completes the net.

A larger double-ended bag can easily be made in the same way for carrying two footballs.

FIG. 150.

Shopping Bag (first design)

The finished bag, when empty will appear as in Fig. 151. When in use it will swell to a surprising degree as indicated by the broken line. It is worked from the bottom towards the mouth. While in the making, therefore, it will be in an inverted position. Near the mouth its circumference is divided first into halves (Fig. 151A and B) and then each half is further divided into two so that the mouth becomes quartered. In the directions for making, these quarters will be referred to as the 1st, 2nd, 3rd, and 4th quarters. (Fig. 151, i, ii, iii, and iv.)

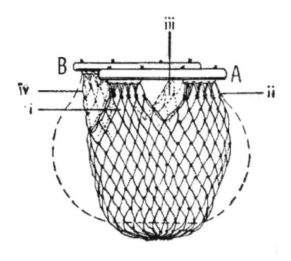

FIG. 151.

Set up by method 3 for bag nets. Use size 7 cotton twine—
or heavier if preferred.

i. Cast on 20 setting-up loops (round 1)—$1\frac{1}{2}$ in. bar.

ii. Make a closed ring and suspend on a toggle.

iii. Make 9 rounds (2–10).

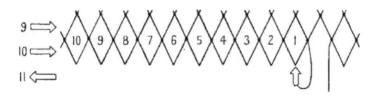

FIG. 152.

163

iv. At the end of the 10th round omit the joining knot on the standing part and return for a distance of 10 meshes—i.e., work a return round (right-to-left) on half the complete circle of meshes (round 11) (Fig. 152). Make straight selvedges.

v. On reaching the 10th mesh change direction again and work, left-to-right, for a distance of 5 meshes (round 12) (Fig. 153).

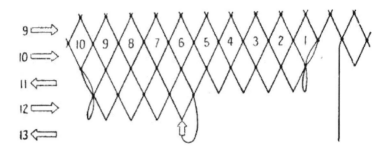

FIG. 153.

vi. After 5 meshes return right-to-left again (round 13) (Fig. 153).

vii. Now double the meshes of round 13 by working left-to-right (Fig. 154), forming the knots on top of the previous ones as described under "doubling". Do not double the small selvedge mesh (*A*) on the right-hand selvedge.[1] This doubling round (14) is indicated by the broken line in the figure. It completes the 1st quarter of the bag.

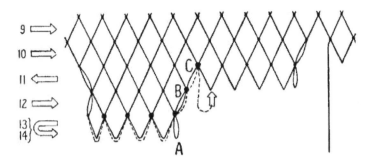

FIG. 154.

viii. When the small selvedge mesh (*A*) is reached (Fig. 154), instead of doubling it, carry the twine up to the end mesh (*B*) of the previous round and form an ordinary netting knot on top of the existing one as indicated by the broken line.

ix. This done continue up to the next round above and make another knot on top of the existing one (Fig. 154, *C*). The selvedge between (*A*) and (*C*) will now consist of small mesh, triple bar, double bar. This is easily followed in the figure.

x. From *C* continue an ordinary round for five meshes to the right to complete round 12 of the second quarter. Make straight selvedges.

165

xi. Return, left-to-right, to make round 13 of the second quarter.

xii. Double over this round as before by working to the right again. Do not double the small selvedge mesh (Fig. 155A). This completes the 2nd quarter.

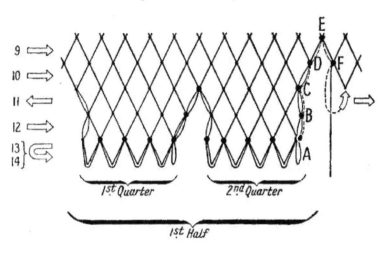

FIG. 155.

xiii. Next work the twine up along the selvedge from *A* to *E* (Fig. 155) as described under viii and ix above, and down the other side to *F* (dotted line).

xiv. Now complete the 3rd and 4th quarters on the meshes of the second half in the same way as quarters (1) and (2) were made on the first half. The arrows on the broken line indicate the beginning of round 11 in the 3rd quarter.

Be sure to include the standing part of the twine in the selvedge knots on the left-hand selvedge of this quarter (see Figs. 146 and 147).

It should be noticed that in making a bag of this kind there must be an even number of meshes in the last complete round (round 10 in this instance) so that it may be divided equally into two. Each half must also consist of an even number of meshes so that it can be further divided into two. The number of meshes in the first dividing round must therefore always be an even number multiplied by 2—e.g., 6 × 2; 8 × 2; 10 × 2; etc. Any number of meshes can be cast on to make the setting-up round provided that the necessary corrections are made by creasing or bating before the first dividing round is reached.

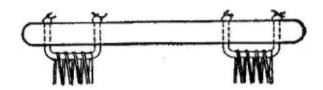

FIG. 156.

Having completed the netting it must be attached to carrying grips. The simplest method is to make two wooden rods, $7\frac{1}{2}$in. long and $\frac{5}{8}$ in. circumference, nicely rounded at the ends. Four holes are bored through each rod, two near each end, $1\frac{1}{2}$in. apart. Through an outermost hole pass a stout cord, lace it through the meshes of the 1st quarter, and pass back through the next hole. Draw tight and knot on the upper side (Fig. 156). Cut off the ends. The meshes of the 2nd quarter are laced on a cord passed through the holes at the other end of the rod. The other side is similarly attached to the second rod and the bag is complete.

Shopping Bag (second design)

Set up by method 3 for bag nets. Use size 6 cotton twine or heavier. Meshes of $1\frac{1}{2}$in. bar.

In this design rings of cane, wood or metal about 3 in. inside diameter are used for carrying handles (Fig. 157). The mouth of the bag is halved, as before, but is not quartered. There are no other differences so there is no change in the manner of working until round 11—the halving round—is reached. Rounds 12 and 13 on each side are worked on the full number of 10 meshes and *not* on 5 + 5 as in the previous design. In making round 13 the mesh gauge is dispensed with and the meshes formed over one of the rings. Double over round 13 in the usual way. The change-over from the first to the second side is made in exactly the same way as in the previous design.

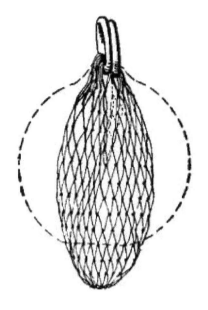

FIG. 157.

Shopping Bag (third design)

In this design circular carrying handles are again used but the bag is "braided flat" and the edges laced together to finish off. Set up 10 meshes on one of the rings by the ordinary setting-up method (method 1). Make a simple piece of flat netting 26 rounds deep and $1\frac{1}{2}$in. bar, and include the second ring in the 26th round. Then fold over, tie the two rings securely together, one on top of the other, and lace the selvedges neatly together leaving three rounds free on each side for the mouth opening. Then cut the rings free again and

169

the bag is complete.

If desired, this bag can be set up by method 2 for sleeve netting using one of the rings instead of a foundation loop. If this method be used the standing part is dispensed with and the netting braided flat in the ordinary way.

Sleeve Net for Net-ball Goal

This is a simple sleeve of netting, open at both ends.

Set up by method 2 for sleeve netting. Use cotton or hemp twine, size 10 or 11; or manila (sisal) 4 ply, 75's.

i. Cast on 15 setting-up loops—2 in. bar.

ii. Make 8 rounds.

iii. Remove foundation loop and lace or marl the setting-up loops evenly on to the goal ring.

If preferred, the net may be set up directly on the goal ring.

A Garden Hammock

Set up by method 1 for flat netting. Use size 7 or 8 cotton twine; or manila (sisal) 4 ply, 100's.

i. Cast on 15 meshes—$2\frac{1}{2}$ in. bar.

ii. Braid ordinary flat netting until 9 ft. long (about 42

rounds). Make straight selvedges.

iii. Marl one selvedge to a good quality rope about $1\frac{1}{2}$ in. in circumference so that the first and last rounds are 8 ft. 6 in. apart when the rope is stretched taut. Leave 2 ft. of extra rope at each end.

iv. Marl the other selvedge to another rope in the same way.

v. Obtain two brass or galvanised rings having an opening 2–3 in. in diameter. Then with an eye-splice attach one end of one of the selvedge ropes to one of the rings leaving 20 in. of free rope between the ring and the end of the hammock netting (Fig. 158).

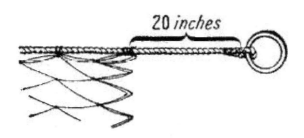

20 *inches*

FIG. 158.

vi. To the same ring similarly attach the other selvedge rope.

vii. With the second ring repeat v and vi at the other end of the hammock.

viii. Make a "stretcher" for the head end of the hammock. This is a wooden bar $36 \times 1\frac{1}{4} \times \frac{3}{4}$in. with a deep notch cut in each end (Fig. 159).

ix. Make a similar stretcher for the foot of the hammock 28 $\times 1\frac{1}{4} \times \frac{3}{4}$in.

FIG. 159.

x. Splice a piece of stout rope, the hammock sling, into each ring; the length of these slings will be governed by the distance apart of the supports from which the hammock is to be slung.

xi. Sling the hammock in a low position and insert the stretchers, one at each end, between the selvedge ropes which fit into the notches in the ends.

xii. Attach one end of a length of twine to the outer mesh of one end of the hammock netting; lead this twine up through the ring, between the selvedge ropes, and back to the second mesh where it can be either knotted, or laced through. Continue until all the end meshes have been taken up in this way (Fig. 160). Repeat at the other

172

end and the hammock is complete.

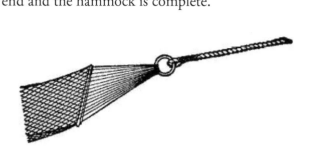

FIG. 160.

A Rabbit (Purse) Net

Set up by method 1 or 3 for flat netting. Use size 2 or 3 cotton twine.

i. Unwind from the needle about 3 ft. of twine to be left free as a spare end.

ii. Cast on 16 loops—2 in. bar.

iii. Make 21 rounds—normal selvedge.

iv. Cut away the needle leaving about 3 ft. of twine attached to the netting.

v. Obtain a light but strong brass ring about $1\frac{1}{4}$ in. internal diameter, and, dispensing with the mesh gauge and needle, make a final row of meshes on this ring, using only the fingers to do so.

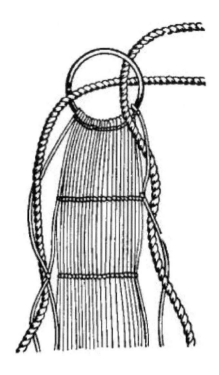

FIG. 161.

vi. Make a secure knot to finish off and cut away the surplus twine.

vii. Release the first row of meshes by removing the foundation line. Invert the netting so that the bottom end, with ring attached, is uppermost and suspend from this ring.

viii. Using the spare end of twine left free when setting up, braid a second brass ring into what was originally the top end of the netting.

ix. Take a length of soft-laid cord, size 6 or 7, and, after passing an end through one ring, reeve it through the selvedge meshes of one side, through the second ring, back through the selvedge meshes on the other side, and through the first ring again (Fig. 161).

x. Stretch the netting to its full length and cut off the two ends of cord about a foot beyond the ring. Attach both to a wooden peg and the net is ready for use.

A Tennis Net

A tennis net is made of square netting and should have a mesh bar of not more than $1\frac{3}{4}$in. Use the method described on using size 7 cotton or 3 ply 120's manila.

i. Start with a single mesh—$1\frac{3}{4}$ in. bar.

ii. Make a series of rounds, inserting a creasing mesh on each selvedge before beginning the next round until a length of $3\frac{1}{2}$ft. is reached along selvedge *A* (Fig. 86. Make straight selvedges (Fig. 87).

iii. Now crease and bate in alternate rounds until a length of 42 ft.[1] is reached along selvedge *B* (Figs. 86; 87). Before beginning to bate, a piece of twine or ribbon of contrasting colour should be tied to the creasing selvedge so that it can always be readily identified. If this is not done the batings and creasings may get mixed up and a zig-zag net will result!

iv. Finish off by bating on both selvedges until only one mesh remains.

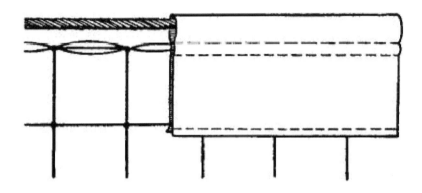

FIG. 162.

v. Sew a canvas band, doubled, along selvedge *B* so as to include the top row of meshes and the metal cable from which the whole is to be suspended. At least three rows of stitching will be needed as indicated by the broken lines in Fig. 162. To comply with the rules of the game the cable must be not more than $\frac{1}{3}$in. in diameter and the canvas band not less than 2 in. nor more than $2\frac{1}{2}$ in. wide.

vi. Fit a vertical strap, not more than 2 in. wide, down the middle of the net for holding it down taut, and the tennis net is ready for use.

Otter Type Fishing Trawls

Many different kinds of nets are used by professional fishermen. Most of these are best obtained ready-made[1] from net-making firms; or suitable netting may be bought in large machine-made pieces that can then be cut to the required size and shape and attached to appropriate mounting ropes, according to their type and purpose. But there is one kind of fishing net, the trawl, that is best braided by hand throughout. It is made in sections that must be suitably shaped to correspond with other parts that have to be joined to them. The batings and creasings required to do this really successfully can be inserted only by hand. It is true that pieces of sheet netting can be cut to shape but the component parts of trawls made in this way lack the necessary slack (provided by extra meshes in certain parts where machines cannot put them) that is essential for the very best fishing.

In spite of its apparent complexity a trawl is really a relatively simple fishing instrument that should commend itself to naturalists, yachtsmen and others wishing to catch fish for scientific purposes, for sport, or simply to add fresh fish to the ship's rations. The naturalist, at any rate, will wish to catch fish for all three reasons.[1]

Fundamentally, a trawl consists of a tapered sleeve of netting—closed at the narrow end—which is towed along the sea floor with its wide end foremost, entrapping fish and other creatures that fail to get out of its way quickly (Fig. 163). Being in contact with the sea bottom the sleeve becomes flattened but remains open so long as it is kept moving. Projecting forwards from each side of the mouth are two long extensions of netting (*A* and *B*) known as the "wings" and indicated by broken lines in the figure. In addition, still another piece of netting—whose forward edge is indicated by the broken line *C*—is carried forward from the upper side of the mouth and attached along its edges to the upper edge of each wing. This part of the trawl, known as the "square," thus forms a large canopy projecting forwards in front of the mouth; without it a trawl would catch very few fish.

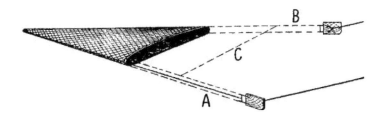

FIG. 163.

For simplicity in braiding, a trawl is formed of separate upper and lower portions laced together at the edges, one row of lacing (the lastrich[1]) being indicated in Fig. 163 by an uneven line up the near side, including the wing, which is thereby divided into upper and lower portions known as the upper wing and lower wing respectively. A similar lastrich (not shown) is present on the other side.

In practice every trawl of any considerable size diverges considerably from the fundamental pattern described above. The square is extended at each side to meet the upper edges of the lower wings and the reduced upper wings extend forward at each side from the front margin of the square. The after ends of the upper wings (Fig. 164) and to a lesser extent those of the lower wings also (Fig. 165) are widened so as to produce a more effective fishing device.

¹ Pronounced "lacestretch" = laced edge.

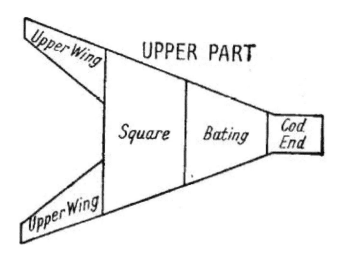

FIG. 164.

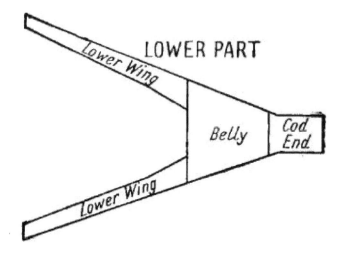

FIG. 165.

Both the upper and lower portions of a trawl are themselves made up of different parts that are braided separately. The lower part consists of a cod end, belly, and lower wings (Fig. 165). The upper portion consists of a cod end identical with the lower one; a piece called the "batings," almost but not quite identical with the corresponding belly of the lower part; the square already referred to above; and the upper wings (Fig. 164).

The forward margins of the upper portion of a trawl—i.e., the upper (inner) edges of the wings and the front edge of the square—are mounted on a light line, the headline, often supported by small floats. The forward margins of the lower portion—i.e., the bottom (inner) edges of the lower wings and the front edge of the belly (the bosom)—are likewise joined to a much heavier rope, the footrope, generally weighted with chains and bobbins. At the forward extremity of the wings, both headline and footrope are attached to wooden "doors" known as "otter boards" or "otter doors" (Fig. 163), which are suitably shod with heavy iron mountings on their lower edges. To these boards the towing warps are attached in such a way that the forward pull of the ship causes them to stand up on edge and set outwards from each other with a kite-like action and thus produce a tension on the headline that serves to keep it taut and well raised above the ground.

There are other kinds of trawls in which the mouth is kept open by a rigid framework but these need not concern us here.

Otter-type trawls and their component parts having now been described, directions for making them should be easily understood. The instructions that follow deal with the braiding of the net only. How to join up the different parts and mount them on the ropes—i.e., how to "fix" a trawl—is an operation that cannot readily be learned from a book but can quickly be picked up from any skilled trawl fisherman.

Small Otter Trawl (suitable for 30 ft. motorboat)

Set up by any of the three methods for ordinary flat netting.

Start with the square.

Square

> Cast on 80 meshes—$2\frac{1}{2}$ in. bar; size 4 cotton. ⎫
> BATE every SIXTH round (both selvedges) ⎬ 10 ft.
>   down to 66 meshes. ⎪
> Continue at 66 till 10 ft. long. ⎭

Upper Wings

These are braided directly on to the head—i.e., the forward edge—of the square; size 4 cotton.

> Take up 25 meshes, beginning at one sel- ⎫
>   vedge—$2\frac{1}{2}$ in. bar. ⎪
> Fly-mesh inner edge—doubled (p. 46). ⎪
> CREASE every SIXTH round on outer selv- ⎬ 16 ft.
>   edge down to 6 meshes. ⎪
> Continue at 6 (CREASE every SECOND[1]) till ⎪
>   16 ft. long. ⎪
> Finish with two rounds double twine. ⎭

Bating

> Cast on 66 meshes—$1\frac{1}{2}$ in. bar; size 4 cotton. ⎫
> BATE every EIGHTH round (both selvedges) ⎬ 21 ft.
>   down to 40 meshes. ⎪
> Continue at 40 till 21 ft. long. ⎭

Cod Ends

Cast on 40 meshes—1½ in. bar ; size 6 cotton. ⎫
Make 8 ft. ⎬ 8 ft.
Finish off with four rows double twine. ⎭

Belly

Cast on 66 meshes—2½ in. bar ; size 4 cotton. ⎫
BATE every EIGHTH round (both selvedges) ⎪
    down to 40 meshes. ⎬ 23 ft.
Continue at 40 till 23 ft. long. ⎭

Lower Mings

These are not usually braided directly on to the belly. A separate piece of netting—the bosom—the same width as the head of the belly and a few rounds deep, is made and the wings are braided on to it. When the trawl is made up this narrow piece with wings attached, is joined to the belly.

Cast on 66 meshes—double twine—2½ in. ⎫
    bar ; size 4 cotton. ⎪
       ⎧ FOUR rounds double ⎫ ⎪
Make SIX ⎨   twine   ⎬ bosom ⎪
  rounds   ⎪ Two rounds single ⎪ ⎪
       ⎩   twine   ⎭ ⎬ 26 ft.
Take up 15 meshes for wing. ⎪
Fly-mesh inner edge—doubled. ⎪
CREASE every THIRD round on outer selv- ⎪
  edge down to 12 meshes. ⎪
Continue at 12 (CREASE every SECOND) till ⎪
  26 ft. long. ⎭

Headline: 16 + 5 + 16 ft. = 37 ft.

Footrope: 23 + 4 + 23 ft. = 50 ft.

Whiting Trawl (Brixham type)

Square

Cast on 400 meshes—1 in. bar ; size 4 cotton. ⎫
BATE every THIRD (both selvedges) down to ⎬ 20 ft.
    250 meshes. ⎪
Continue at 250 till 20 ft. long. ⎭

Upper Wings

Take up 140 meshes for bunt—1 in. bar ; ⎫
    size 4 cotton. ⎪
Work inner selvedge on losing halver by ⎪
    doubling method (p. 34). ⎪
CREASE every SIXTH on outer ⎫ down ⎬ 20 ft.
    selvedge. ⎬ to 20 ⎪
Make an inner BATING every ⎪ meshes ⎪
    SIXTH near inner selvedge. ⎭ ⎪
Continue at 20 (CREASE every SECOND) till ⎪
    20 ft. long. ⎭

Bating

Cast on 250 meshes—1 in. bar. ⎫
BATE every THIRD (both selvedges) down to ⎬ 20 ft.
    100 meshes ⎪
Continue at 100 till 20 ft. long. ⎭

Belly

Cast on 200 meshes.

$$\text{Bate every \textsc{third} (both selvedges)} \left\{ \begin{array}{l} 7\frac{1}{2} \text{ rounds to 1 ft. down} \\ \text{to 160 meshes.} \\ 8\frac{1}{2} \text{ rounds to 1 ft. down} \\ \text{to 120 meshes.} \end{array} \right.$$

Then BATE every FOURTH—10 rounds to 1 ft.
—down to 100 meshes.
Continue at 100 till 22 ft. long.

} 22 ft.

Lower Wings

Cast on 200 meshes for bosom—7½ rounds to 1 ft.
Make several rounds (double twine).
Take up 65 meshes for bunt.
Work inner selvedge on losing halver by doubling method.
CREASE every THIRD on outer selvedge down to 30 meshes.
Continue at 30 till 42 ft. long.

} 42 ft.

Cod Ends

Cast on 100 meshes—10 rounds to 1 ft.
BATE every SECOND (both selvedges) down to 60 meshes.
Continue at 60 till 16 ft. long.

} 16 ft.

Headline: 21 + 7 + 21 ft. = 49 ft.

Footrope: 36 + 6 + 36 ft. = 78 ft.

[1] For a good general survey of British fishing implements reference should be made to "An Account of the Fishing Gear of England and Wales." By F. M. Davis. H.M.S.O. 6/-.

[1] This would produce a treble knot which would be too large and unsightly. Doubled knots are indicated by large dots.

[1] Doubles court size: for a singles court the length should be 33 ft.

[1] Pre-fabricated is perhaps the more fashionable, modern term.

[1] Not everyone knows, though many suspect, that most kinds of fish taste best when their transference from the sea to frying pan or casserole is carried out with the least possible loss of time. This does not apply to soles, which improve on keeping for a reasonable time before cooking, nor to the various species of rays and skates. The latter, if eaten soon after capture, are tough and have a rather bitter taste. If rations are short and they must be cooked quickly, the edible portions

(the wings) should be cut off and the skin of the upper side removed. The skinned wings should then be strung on to a stout line and towed after the ship for several hours. This removes the slime and certain excretory products that lodge in the muscles of these fish and spoil the flavour. If rays and skates cannot be towed behind the ship they should be kept for from one to several days—according to season, i.e., longer in colder weather—before eating. Best of all, the wings should be both towed and kept for a day or two; they will then prove really delicious if properly cooked.

[1] Since fly-meshing loses one mesh in every two rows, creasing every second row on the opposite selvedge keeps the mesh number constant.

CHAPTER VIII

PRESERVATION OF NETS

ALL ropes, twines, cords, strings, threads and the like are perishable whether braided into nets or not. The rate at which they wear out depends upon the kind of fibre from which they are made up and the use to which they are put. Their life can be lengthened by appropriate treatment with preservatives designed to reduce deterioration the chief causes of which are:—

1. *Rotting* due to the action of moulds and bacteria which produce chemical substances that weaken and eventually destroy the fibres.

2. *Mechanical wear and tear* caused by the rubbing of the threads and their component fibres against one another and against external objects with which they come into contact.

3. *Heating* due to oxidation either of the substance of the fibres themselves or (more usually) of organic matter such as fish slime with which the nets may become coated.

188

Tanning or "Barking"

To reduce deterioration due to rotting caused by moulds and bacteria various tanning materials have long been used. The tanning or "barking" process consisted originally of soaking the nets in a hot-water decoction of the barks of certain trees such as oaks, birches, spruces, mangroves and various others. In course of time it became possible to buy convenient extracts of those barks and woods, and from them tanning liquids could more easily be made by simple solution in cold or hot water. Chief amongst those extracts, most of which are still available, are:—

1. Burma cutch or catechou—from the wood of a tree called *Acacia catechu* found in India and Burma.

2. Red or mangrove cutch—from the barks of various mangrove trees.

3. Canada cutch—from the Canadian pine *Abies canadensis.*

4. Quercitron—from the bark of a large N. American timber oak, *Quercus velutina.*

5. Quebracho—from several kinds of S. American trees.

The active principle in all these and various other tanning materials appears to be the tannins that they contain. But they are not ideal preservatives because their preservative properties, at best, are not very great, and they possess the added disadvantage that they are fairly soluble in water. They therefore quickly leach out of nets that are constantly being wetted—e.g., fishing nets—so that "dipping" must be regularly and frequently repeated. This not only involves a lot of time and trouble but is also unsatisfactory for the further reason that tanning materials cause shrinkage of the twine, thus reducing the mesh sizes. Cotton nets, in particular, continue to shrink every time they are "barked"—so much so that old fishing nets may have to be discarded before they are worn out because the twine has become too hard and the meshes too small, even though allowance for shrinkage has been made by starting off with meshes rather larger than are required.

Cutch and Bichromate Treatment

In order to make the tanning materials stay longer in the fabric some makers and users treat nets, that have been fully barked and thoroughly dried, to further soaking in a solution of potassium bichromate which acts as a fixing agent or mordant; i.e., the bichromate renders certain of the tanning substances insoluble in water so that they are less readily leached out of the fabric. The process, which consists of two parts, is as follows:—

A

1. Make up a solution of cutch[1] in water—$\frac{3}{4}$ lb. cutch to 1 gal. hot water.

2. Thoroughly soak the net in the hot "cutch water" for a few minutes.

3. Remove the net from the cutch and suspend it above the container to allow surplus liquid to drain off.

4. Spread the-net out to dry.

5. If the net is new, repeat 2, 3 and 4 once or even twice until a good rich colour is obtained.

B

1. Make up a separate solution of potassium bichromate by boiling in clean water—$\frac{1}{4}$ lb. bichromate to 1 gal. water.

2. Immerse the cutched and dried net in the hot bichromate solution. Stir the net around with a stick to ensure even penetration of the solution into all parts of the fabric; remove and dry. If the bichromate has acted properly the net will now be nearly black.

A net that is kept dry should not require repetition of this treatment for many years. Fishing nets that are constantly wet should be cutched again after every six weeks or two months of regular use—i.e., dipped once in hot cutch of normal strength and dried. Treatment with the bichromate need not be repeated more than once in every twelve to twenty-four months.

It is important to note that the cutch and bichromate

solutions must not be mixed, nor the order of their application reversed. It is also necessary to ensure that cutched nets are dry before the bichromate is applied.

Considerable claims have from time to time been made for the effectiveness of the cutch-bichromate method. It appears, however, to be now generally accepted that, although the colour imparted to them by this process will not readily wash out, the nets are no better preserved than with cutch alone. The method is described here because there may be some who still will wish to use it—but it is not recommended.

Dr. Olie's (Dutch) Method

A real improvement upon the cutch and the cutch-bichromate treatments was devised by a Dr. Olie of the Netherlands about thirty years ago. This, the so-called Dutch treatment, is carried out as follows, again in two parts:

A

1. Make up a cutch solution as previously described.

2. Boil the nets in the cutch water for $\frac{1}{2}$ hr., using enough liquid to cover the nets.

3. Stop boiling after $\frac{1}{2}$ hr. and allow the nets to stay in the liquid for 24 hrs. Then remove and dry thoroughly.

4. Repeat 2 and 3 (one repetition is usually enough).

B

1. Make up a solution of copper sulphate (blue vitriol)—1 lb. blue vitriol to 10 gal. cold water.

2. Add ammonia solution slowly to the copper sulphate solution. A precipitate is first formed.[1] Keep on adding just enough ammonia to redissolve the whole of the precipitate. This will produce a clear deep blue liquid.

3. Place the cutched and dried net in this solution for 10 to 15 mins.—not more.

4. Remove and dry.

Retreatment of nets preserved by the Dutch process is necessary only after about four months continuous use in water. This method is quite successful and can be recommended. Like the others already described, however, it possesses the serious disadvantage of causing marked shrinkage of the fabrics, especially cottons.

Copper Soaps

Investigations by Atkins, Warren and others in this country and by Taylor and Wells in America, have shown that certain compounds of copper—copper oleate, copper resinate, copper naphthenate[1] and a substance known as mixed copper soap—are very good preservatives for all kinds of ropes and netting and cause little shrinkage. Of these, copper naphthenate is the best for general use and is now generally obtainable in this country as a proprietary product called *Cuprinol*. For all ordinary purposes, therefore, treatment with *Cuprinol* is strongly recommended. There are various grades of *Cuprinol*, including one specially prepared for preservation of nets, particularly fishing nets. Net *Cuprinol* contains a certain amount of tar in addition to copper naphthenate. The tar acts as an extra binding medium for the copper salts; it provides only negligible mechanical protection such as is given by tar alone (see below). This preservative imparts a green colour to nets and ropes.

Copper naphthenate and the other copper soaps are particularly good preservatives because in addition to slowing down the processes of deterioration due to moulds and bacteria they also act as a lubricant, reducing internal mechanical wear and tear caused by rubbing of the component fibres against one another as they stretch and contract under the varying strains that are put upon them. Preservation by these substances has also the added advantage that the copper compounds are relatively insoluble in water and therefore leach out of the fabric only very slowly and the beneficial effects of one treatment last a long time.

Copper naphthenate in the proprietary form of *Cuprinol* can be purchased from any ship chandler, paint or hardware store. For all except very fine nets *Cuprinol* can be used without dilution. But for very fine nets in which loss of flexibility must be kept to a minimum it may be found advantageous to dilute the *Cuprinol* with petrol. The amount of dilution will be determined by the result that is desired. Materials treated with *Cuprinol* can be stored for a short time in a damp or wet condition without harm. *Cuprinol* and the other copper soaps also provide effective protection against white ants and other pests found in the tropics.

Copper naphthenate, especially in its proprietary form of *Cuprinol* is expensive. Copper oleate is nearly as good in every way for nets and is very much cheaper: 1lb. of the oleate, together with 1lb tar, in 1 gal. petrol makes a suitable solution. For ropes this solution is less successful as it does not penetrate well into thick fabrics. *Cuprinol*, on the other hand, penetrates rapidly and completely into very thick ropes and should always be used for them. Ropes up to 2-in. circumference require immersion for only 12 to 24 hours in *Cuprinol* as against several days or even weeks in ordinary preservatives. The thin twines of most nets are completely saturated by *Cuprinol* in a few minutes and by ordinary copper soap solution in less than half an hour.

Tar

In a few kinds of net, such as fishing trawls, mechanical wear and tear are the chief causes of deterioration. For such nets, physical protection of the fabric is called for and is best provided by treatment with tar. The wood tars[1] and coal tar are almost equally suitable. The netting may simply be steeped for a few hours in hot tar, hung up over the container until freed from excess, and then spread out to dry. An alternative method is to thin the tar with benzol (instead of thinning by heating) and apply cold. Nets tarred in this way will dry more quickly than those immersed in the tar thinned only by heating.

Treatment with tar fills up the spaces between the fibres and actually increases their strength by gluing them together. A strong tough skin is also formed on the outside of the netting which not only protects the fabric from external abrasion but also prevents water from coming into contact with it—in other words tar helps to keep the net dry even when immersed in water. Nevertheless, tar is not a perfect preservative because it has the disadvantage of considerably increasing the weight of the netting and also of making it rather stiff and rigid so that there is some danger of breakage at the knots where the fibres are sharply bent. This rigidity can be reduced by adding some copper soap[2] to the benzol-tar mixture, in the proportion of one pound of soap to each gallon.

Other Preservatives

Other preservatives used for "curing" nets need not be described at length as they are all relatively unimportant. Creosote[1] (or pickle) is much used in Cornwall and some other places for drift nets. These are usually first cutched and dried, then soaked in "pickle," the excess squeezed out, and the nets then spread out to dry. Or the nets may be passed straight from hot cutch to the pickle. Sometimes a mixture of tar and creosote is used. In whatever way it is applied, creosote has certain disadvantages, the most important of which is that it dries slowly and leaves the net for a long time soft and greasy. Creosoted fishing nets should therefore be dried for a long time before use or the fish they catch may become contaminated with traces of the preservative which has an unpleasant taste. Creosoted nets should be cutched afterwards from time to time. This has a drying effect; in fact it is said that a creosoted net never gets into really good condition until its second season.

Linseed oil, either raw or boiled (or a mixture of both), is also sometimes used for curing nets. The nets are usually first cutched and dried before soaking in the oil until saturated. They are then spread out to dry. It is important that they be fully spread, for if bunched up in lumps much heat is generated and the nets will be ruined. Ideally, the drying process should be carried out in a good current of air in dry and cool weather.

General Care

Nets should never be stored away wet. If they have been used in salt water they should, if possible, be first washed in clean fresh water and then dried thoroughly. Washing is particularly necessary if the nets are covered with fish slime or other organic matter the oxidation of which may generate enough heat to destroy the netting. One of the beneficial effects of dipping fishing nets in hot cutch is that this treatment removes the slime and oil derived from fish and therefore reduces the danger of heating. No preservative is any protection against damage by heat when heating does take place.

As a temporary safeguard, when it is not possible to dry nets that have to be stowed away in small space—e.g., on board a small fishing boat—a good sprinkling of common salt is advisable. Salt helps to keep the temperature down by preventing decomposition and also by extracting heat from its surroundings in the process of dissolving.

Small nets, such as shopping bags, used only or chiefly for purely domestic purposes, will generally be kept quite dry. On the rare occasions when they do get wet they will seldom remain wet for long. Preservative treatment for such nets is quite unnecessary. They should be dyed in bright and attractive colours with any of the usual household dyes that can be bought anywhere for only a few pence. The directions on the packet should be followed—exactly as if dyeing an article of clothing or other domestic fabric.

During the last few years nylon has come into fairly general use for the making of ropes and twines, and nets of many kinds are now braided from nylon materials. Nylon is resistant to the action of moulds and bacteria, and to most chemicals in common industrial use. Treatment with preservative and careful drying before storage are both unnecessary. Nylon does not swell in water nor become hard and intractable when wet. Its great tensile strength and elasticity make it particularly suitable for many exacting purposes. In addition to all its other good qualities nylon will readily "take" most ordinary dyes without losing its characteristic silky sheen. A wide range of useful articles, hard-wearing and of most pleasing appearance, can therefore be made from it.

[1] "Caldacutch," a proprietary brand sold by Beetons Ltd., Sunrise Net Works, Lowestoft, is as good as any.

[1] In other words, the solution becomes cloudy.

[1] Copper naphthenate was first used in Denmark before 1914, and used extensively.

[1] Generally sold as Stockholm tar and Archangel tar. Hardwood tars are obtainable from Messrs. Shirley, Aldned

& Co., Oakwood Chemical Works, Worksop.

² Prepared by Lever Bros, and obtainable from any of the usual drysalters and ship chandlers; or it may be ordered direct from Wm. Bailey & Son, Horsley Field Works, Wolverhampton.

¹ "Tectal," a trade name for a high-boiling creosote, is much used in Northern Ireland.